Barn Owl Photobook:
Royalty Free Color Pix of the Common Barn Owl, Family Tytonidae (Tyto Alba) Plus Talons & Owl Drawings

SHARON BUYDENS

Copyright © 2018 Author Name

All rights reserved.

ISBN: 1718729499
ISBN-13: 978-1718729490

DEDICATION

For Kira.

CONTENTS

1 BARN OWL FACTS 1
2 YOUNG 2
3 WATCHING 4
4 LEFT 8
5 RIGHT 14
6 OWLNESS 19
7 COLOR 24
8 TALONS 30
9 SLEEPY 33
10 WINGS 35
11 ARTWORK 38

ACKNOWLEDGMENTS

Many thanks to the Creative Commons. I am happy to pass along these royalty-free images for everyone. Images in this book can be used for any personal/commercial purpose without attribution.

1 BARN OWL FACTS

- The common barn owl (Tyto alba) is one of the most widespread birds, so it not endangered. The family is Tytonidae (the other lineage of owls is Strigidae, a typical or "true owl"). Barn owls are found most everywhere except extremely hot and cold climates.

- The size of the barn owl is usually medium with a pale color, long wings, and a short square tail. Size is quite variable in subspecies, ranging from 13-15 inches (33-39 cm) or even as short as 11 inches (29 cm) or as long as 17 inches (44 cm). Wing spans range from 21-41 inches (68-105 cm), with average wingspans of 31-37 inches (80-95 cm). Subspecies can vary even more, including in coloring. Barn owls weigh about 9.2 oz (260 g) to 19.6 oz (555 g).

- The barn owl's face is usually white and heart-shaped, and their call is a long shriek, which sounds different than a typical owl hoot. They are nocturnal so hunt at night (except in some of the Pacific Islands and in Britain, where they hunt during the daytime). Their hearing is very acute so they can locate small animals to hunt by sound. The owls mate for life, unless one dies, and then the surviving owl may find another mate to bond with. The female incubates the eggs while the male finds them food.

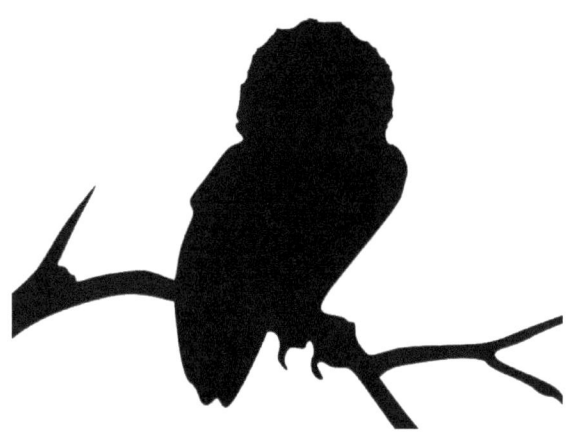

2 YOUNG

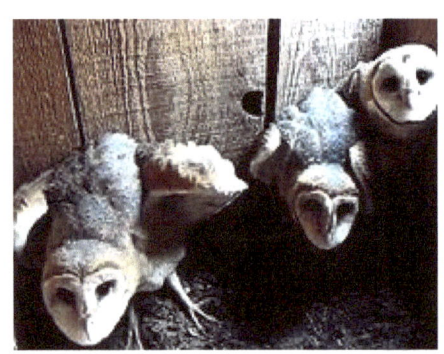 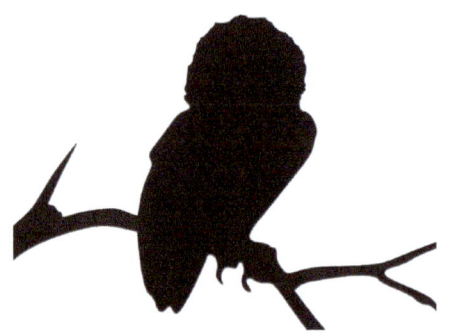

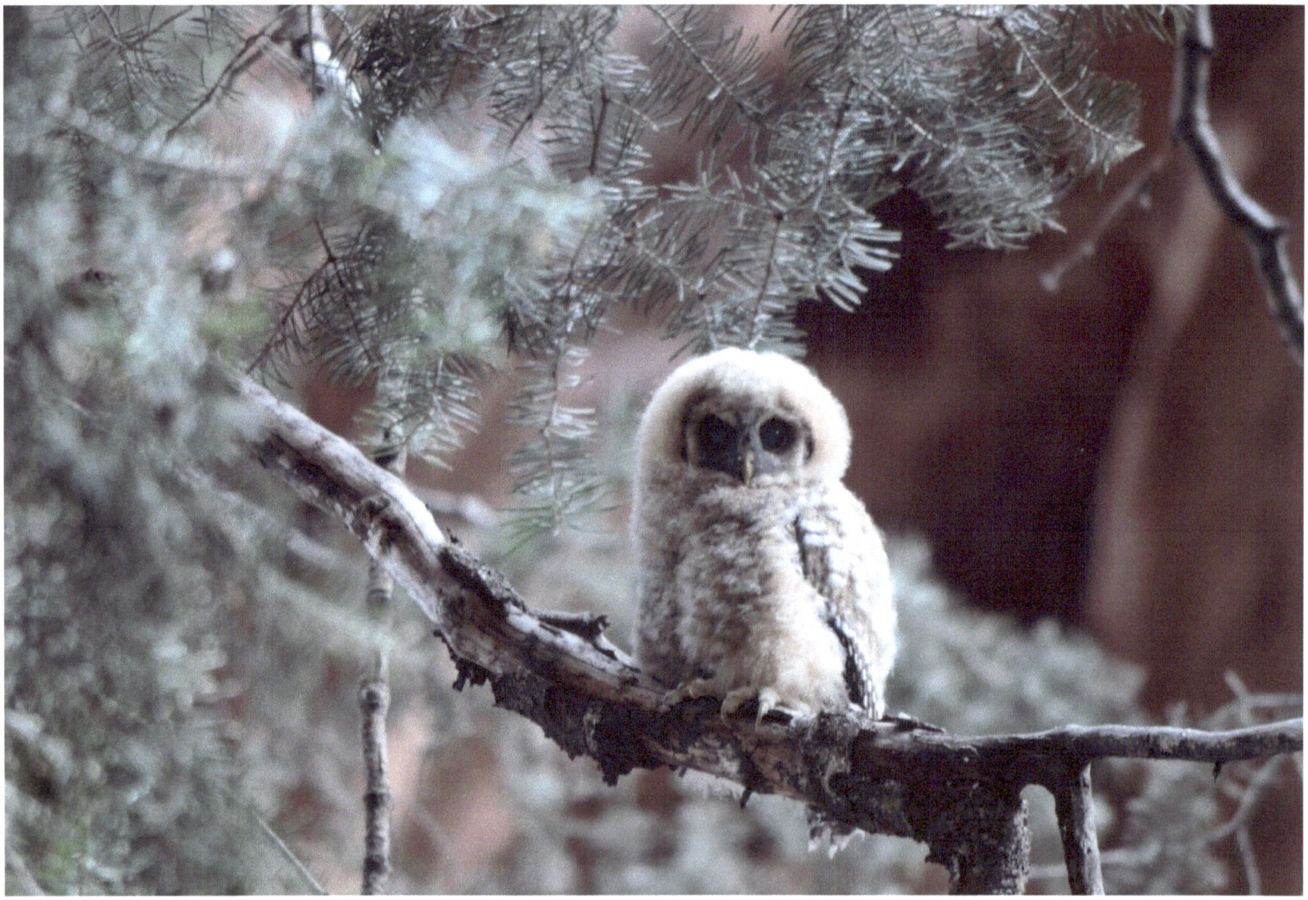

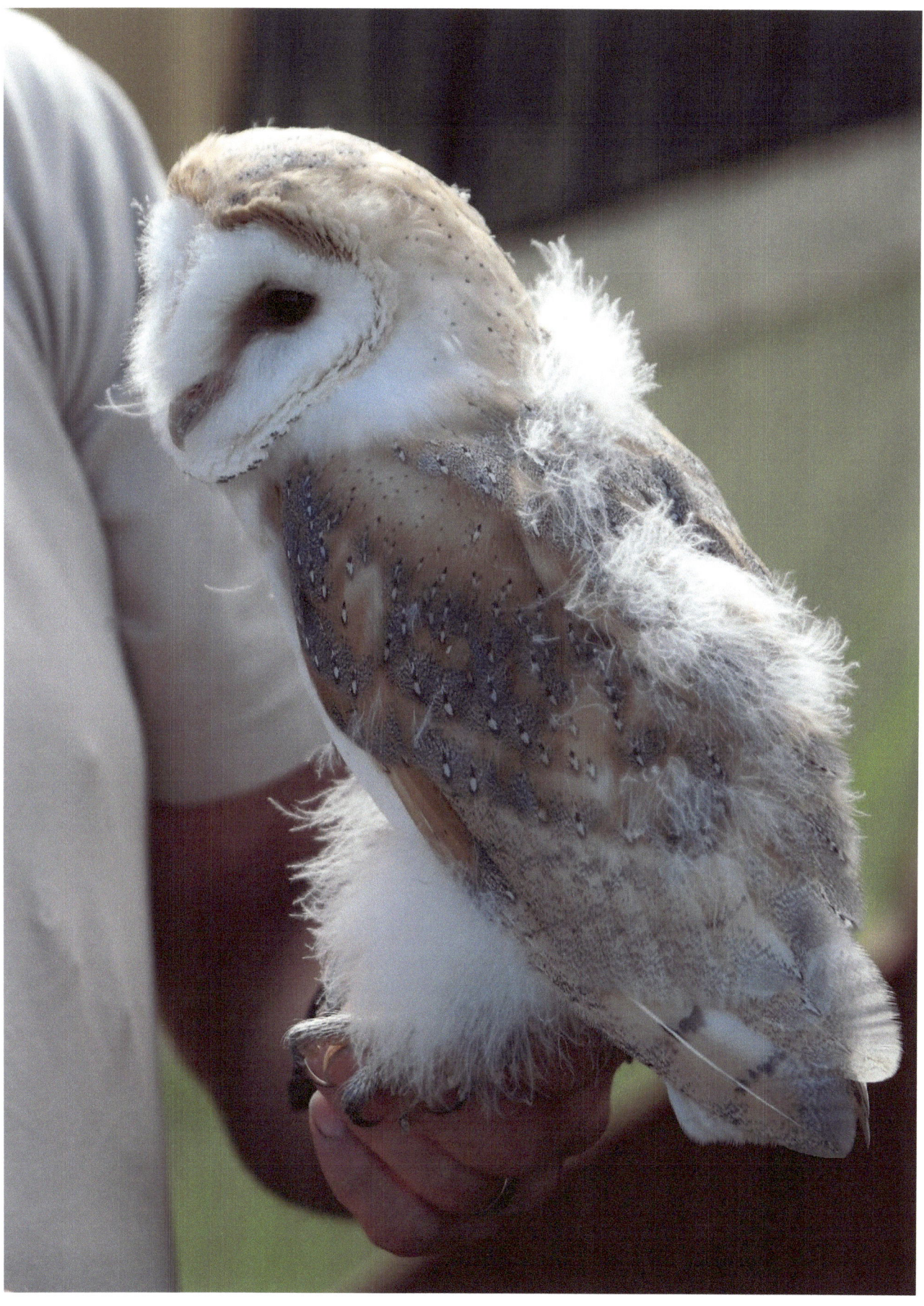

3 WATCHING

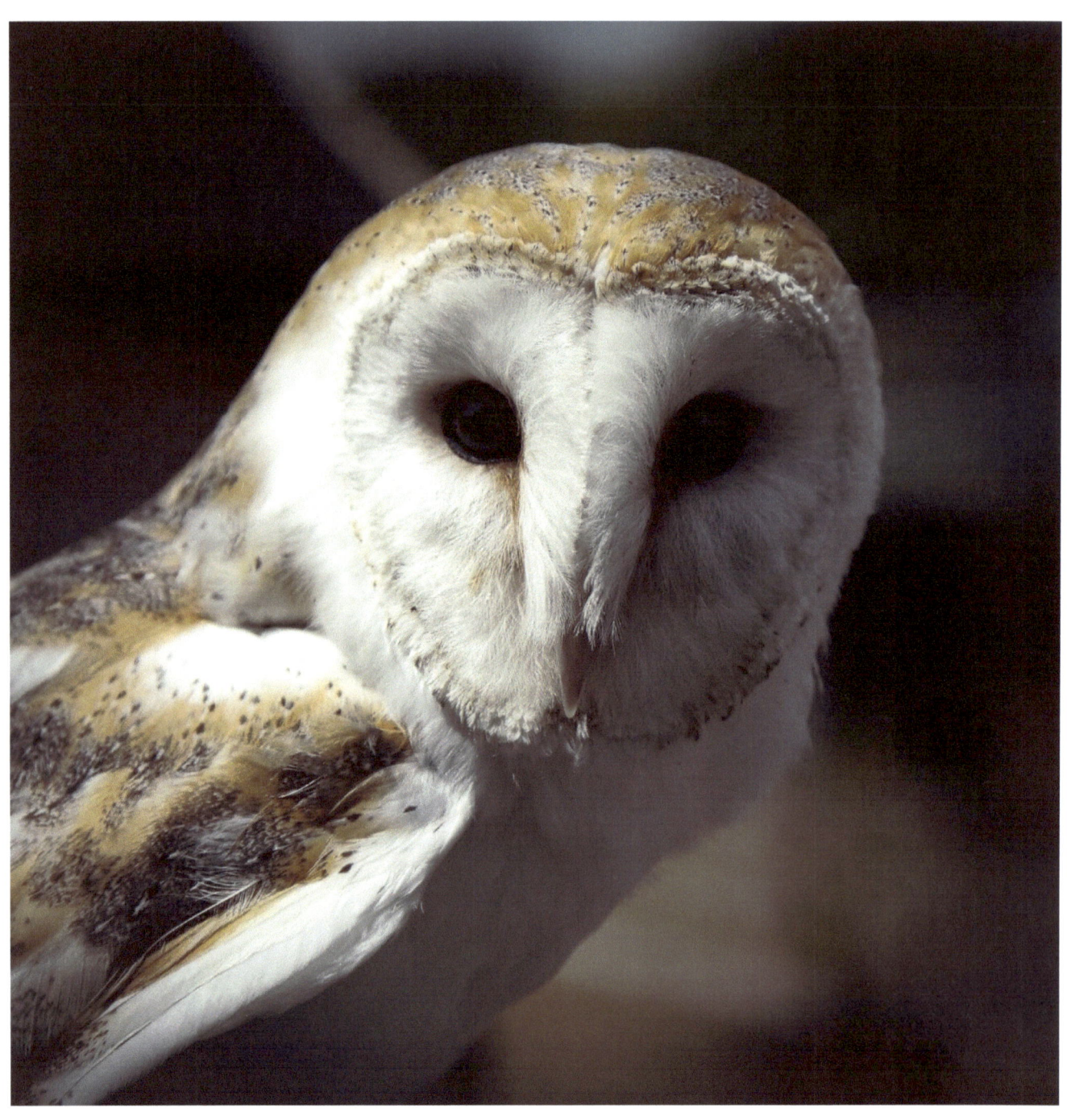

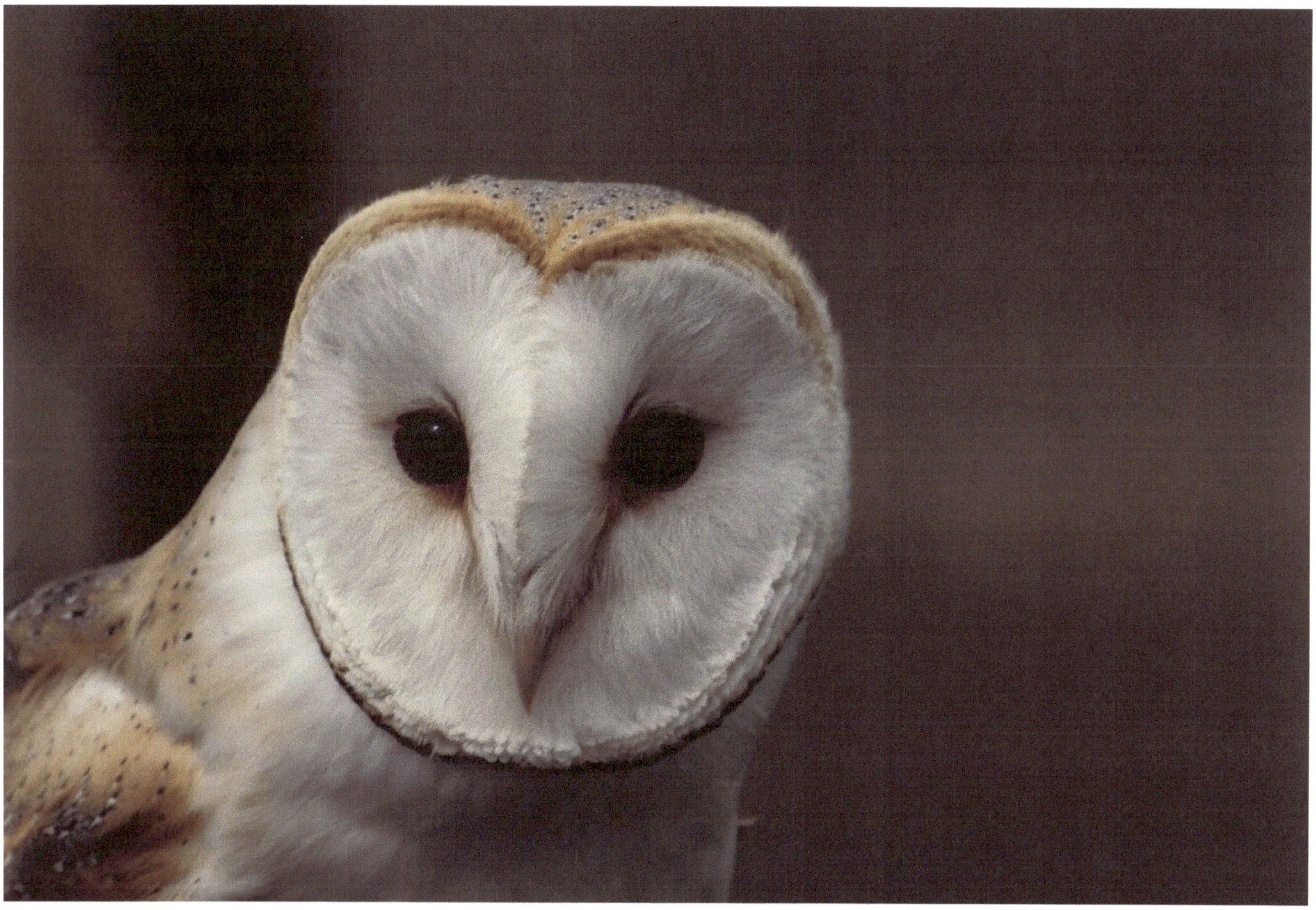

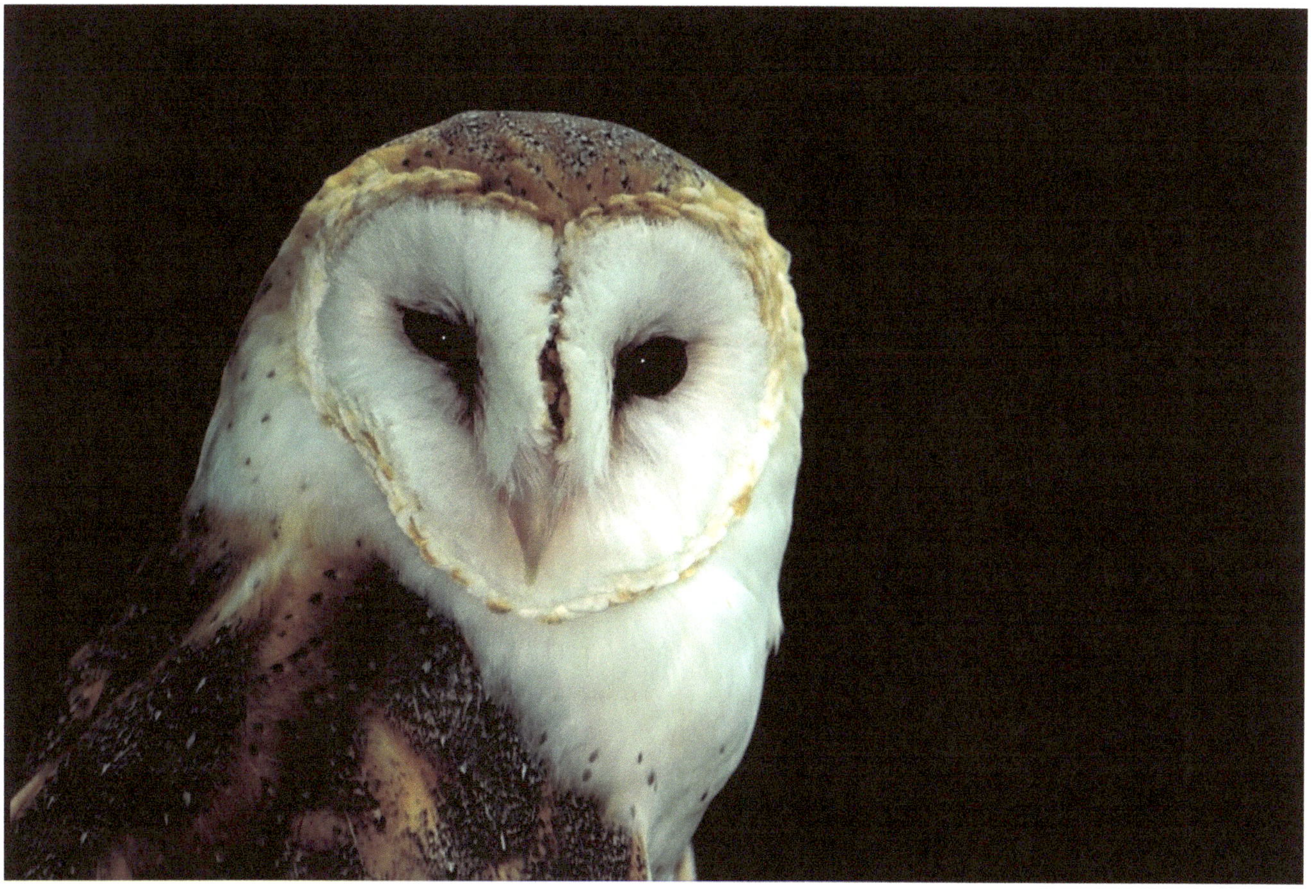

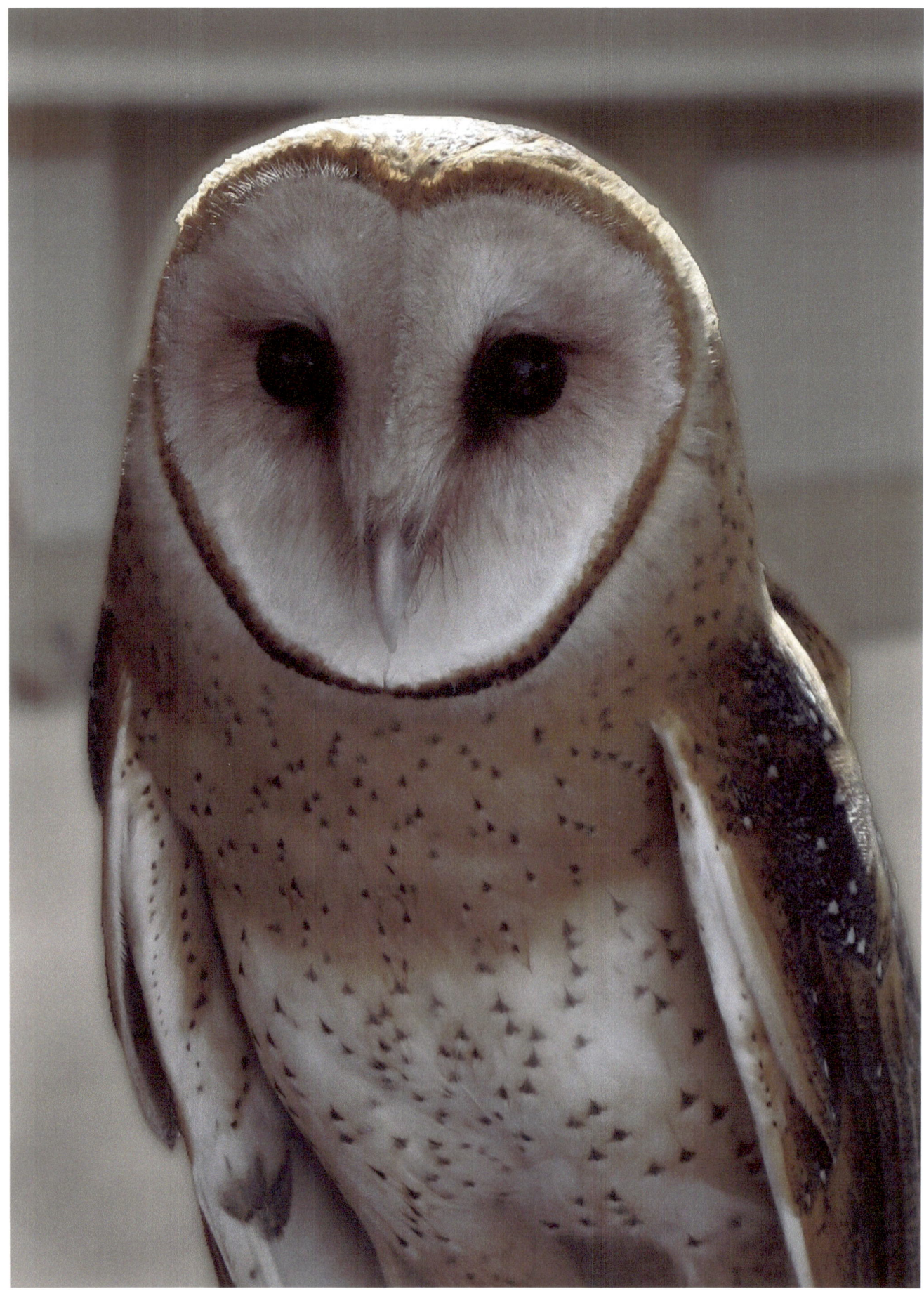

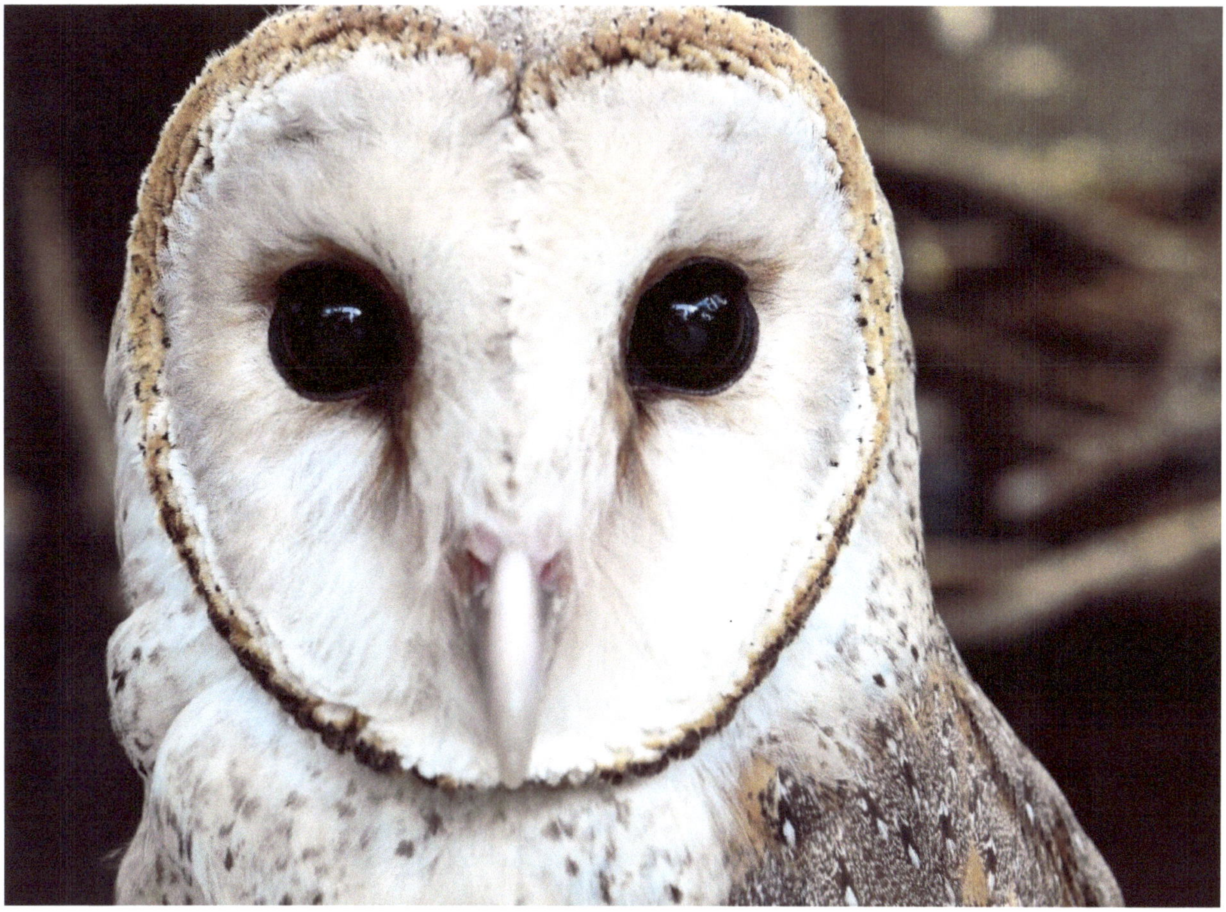

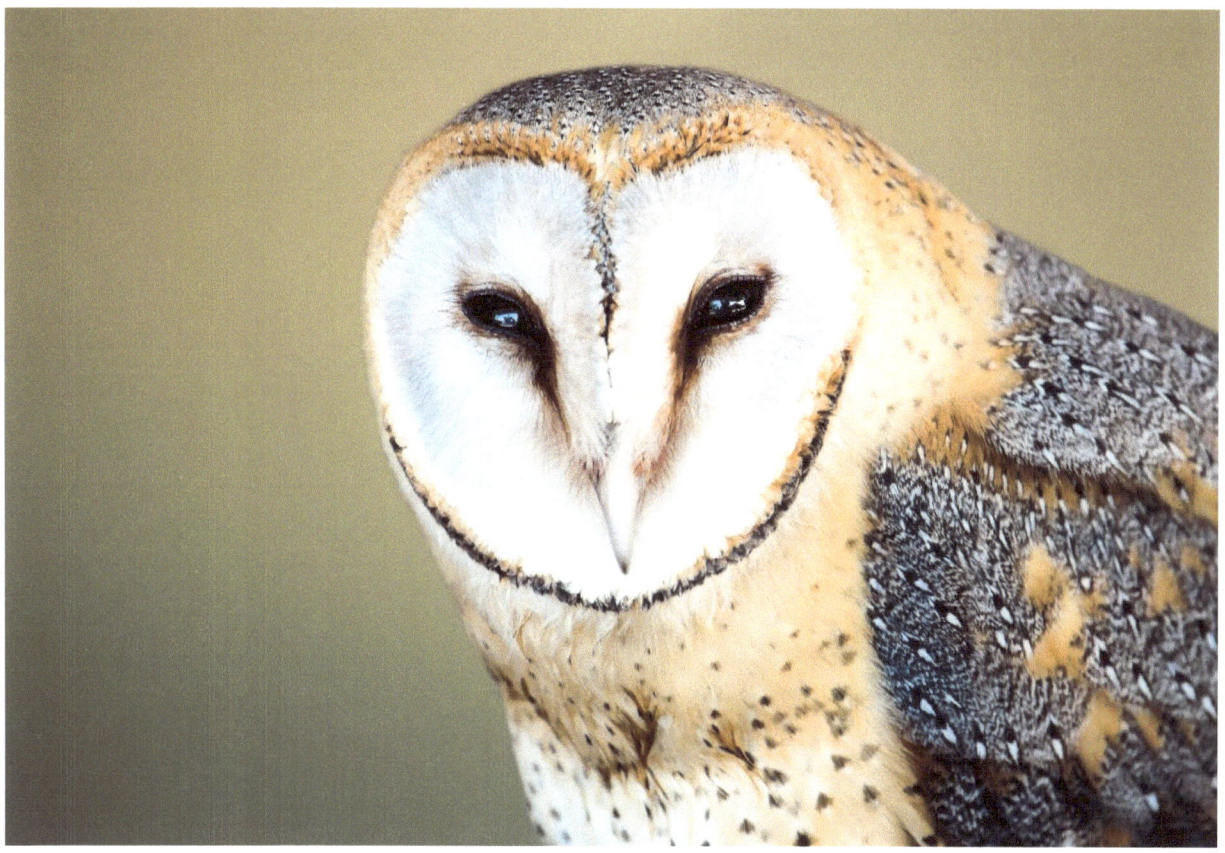

4 LEFT

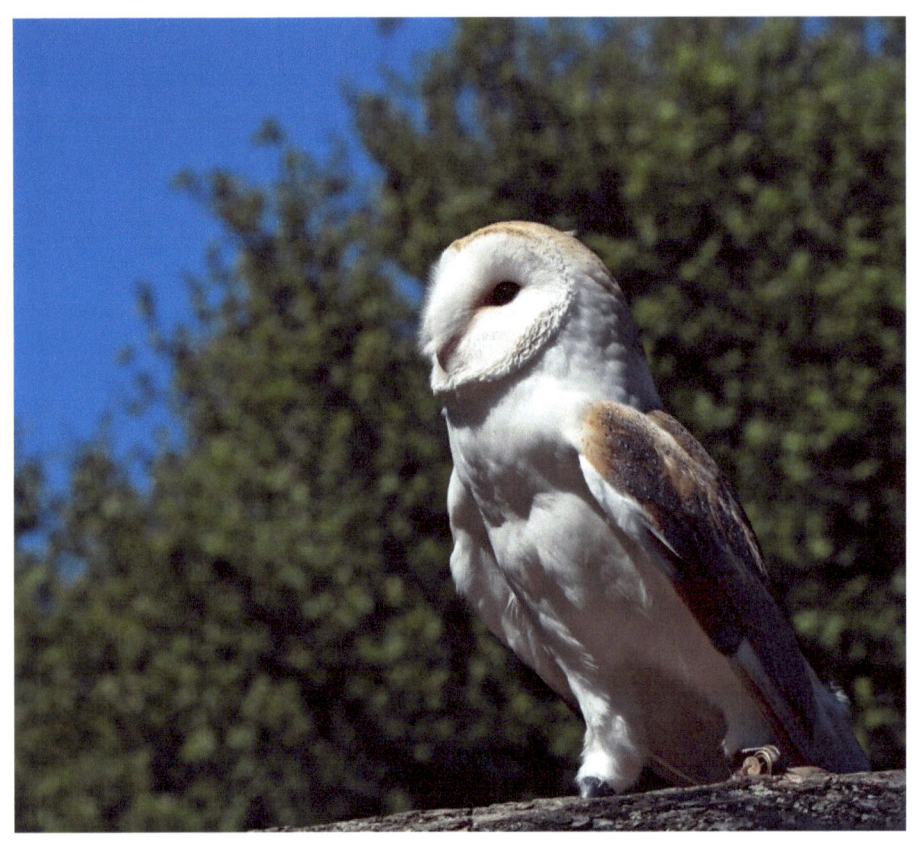

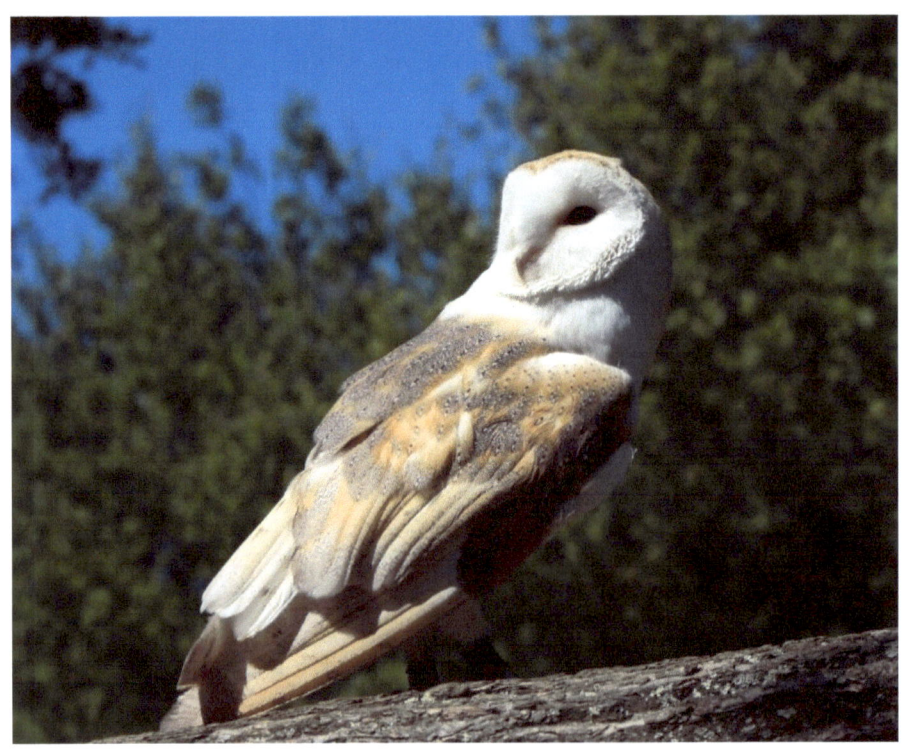

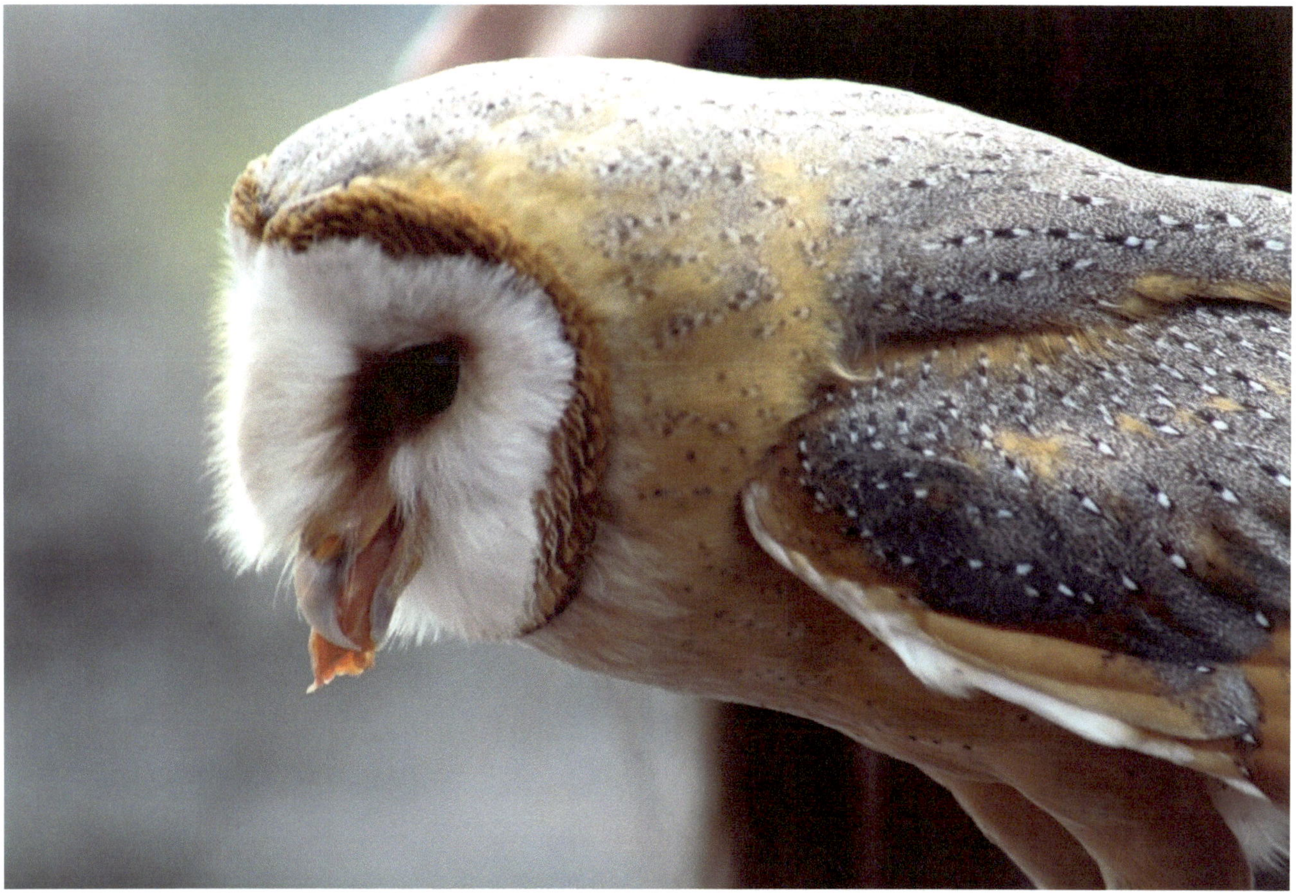

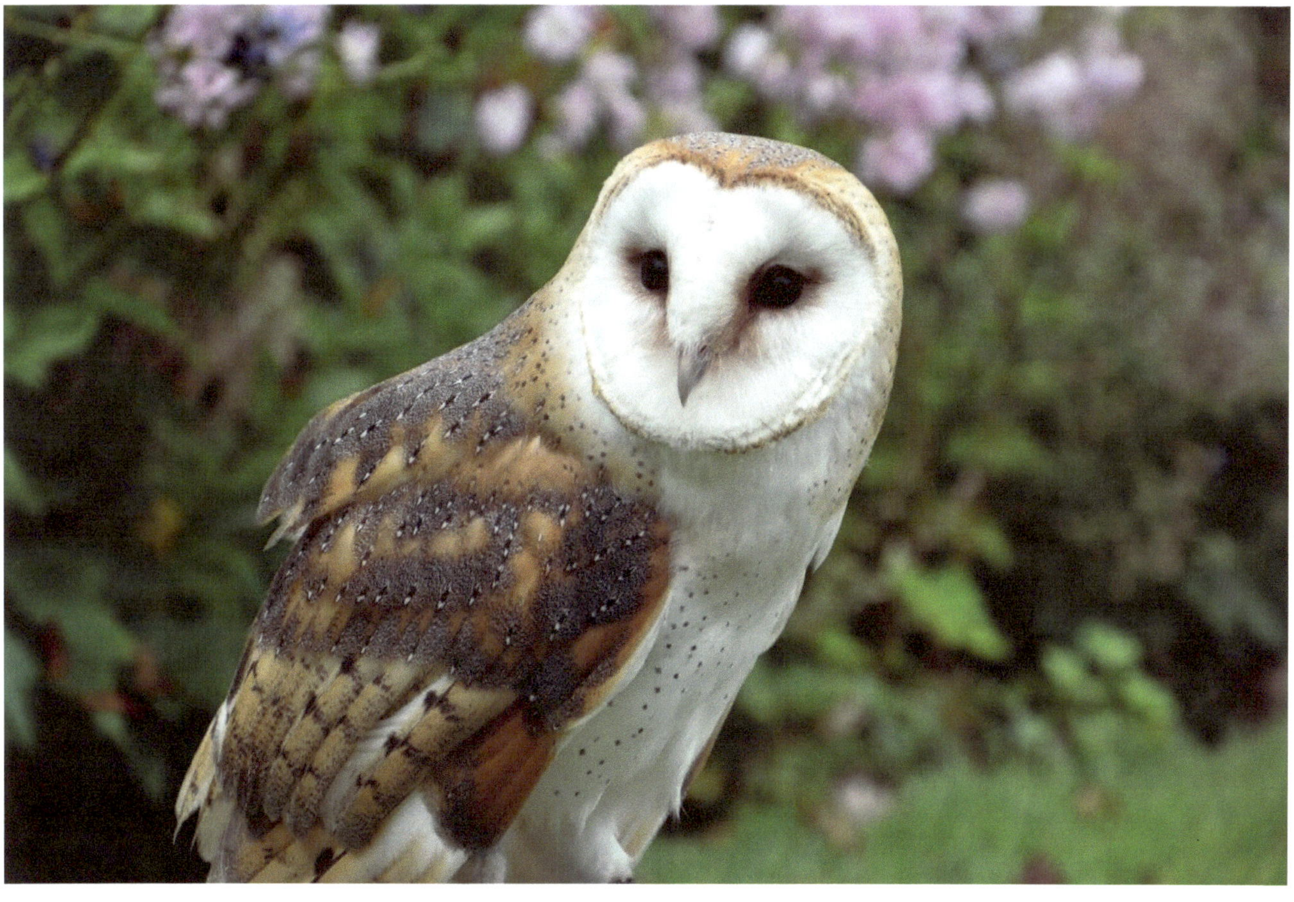

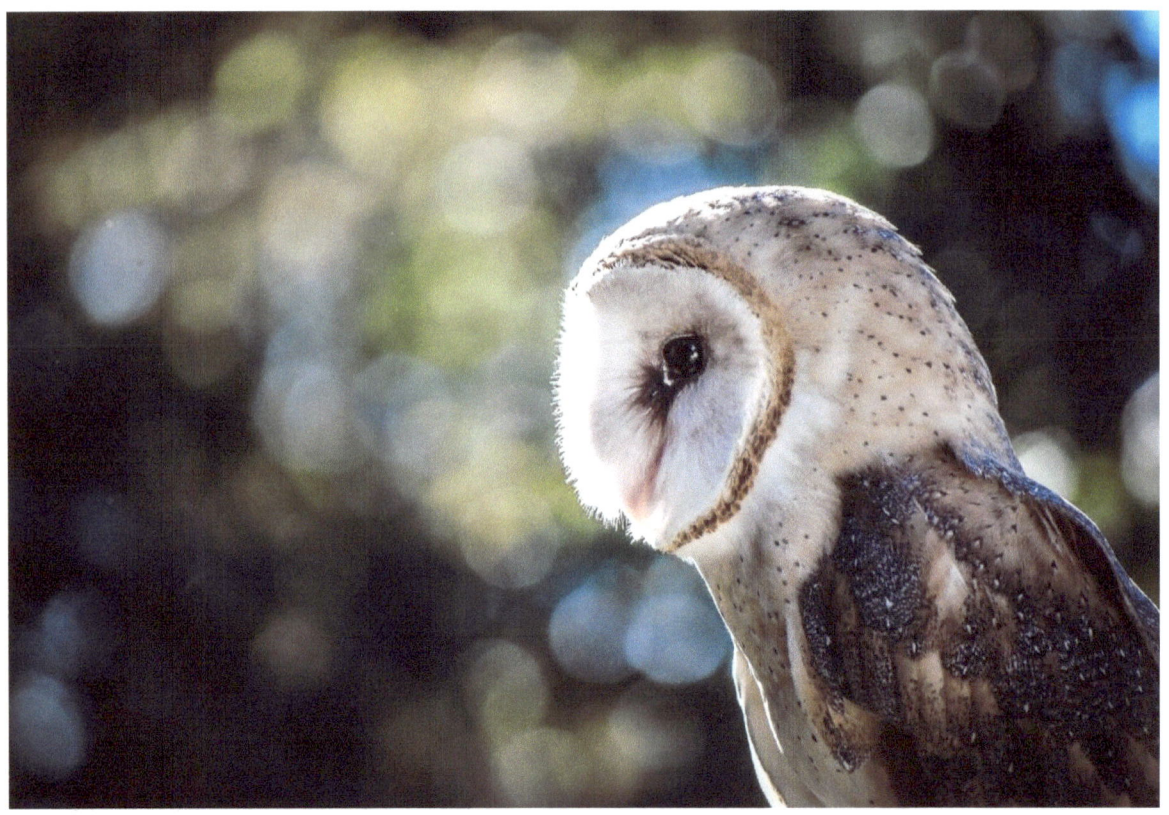

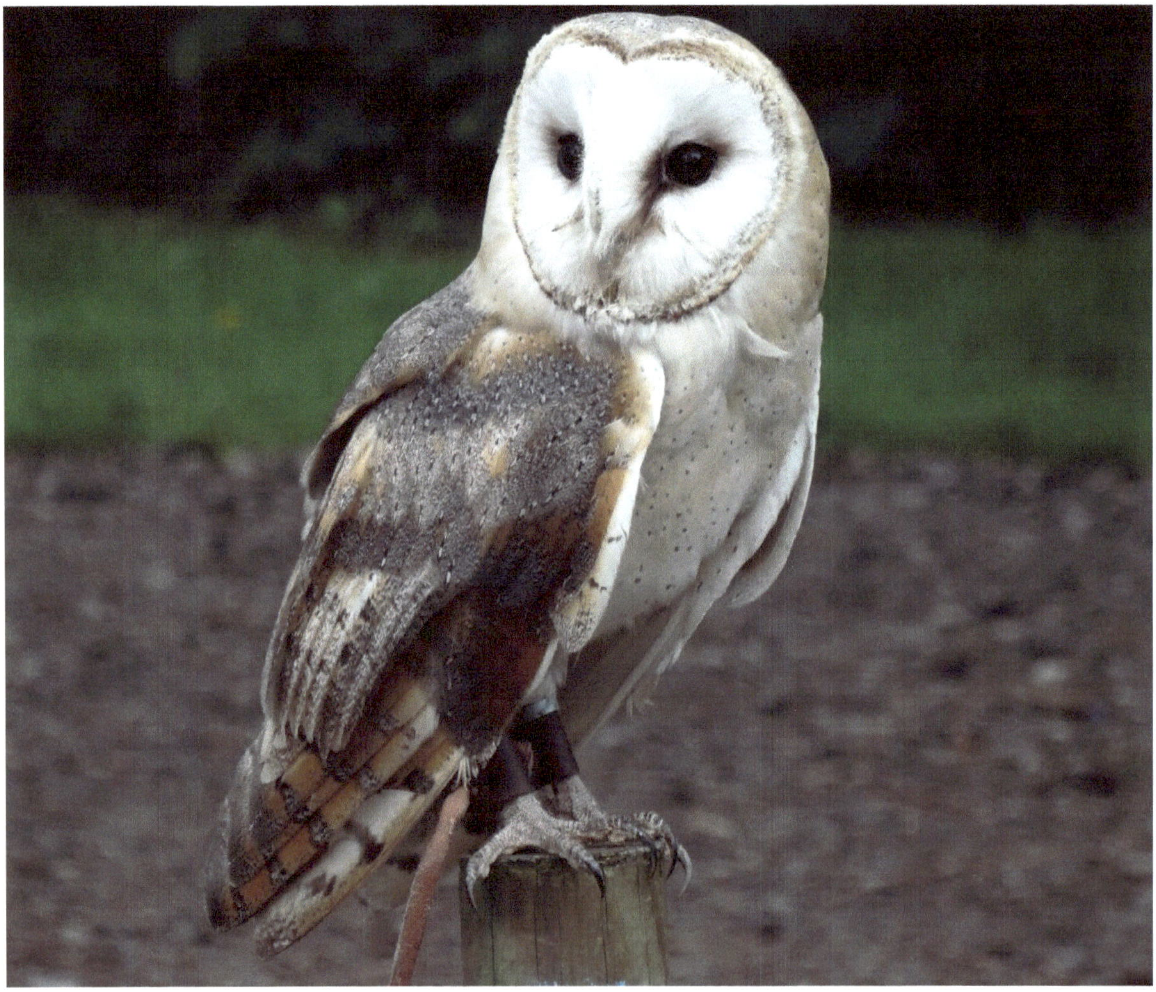

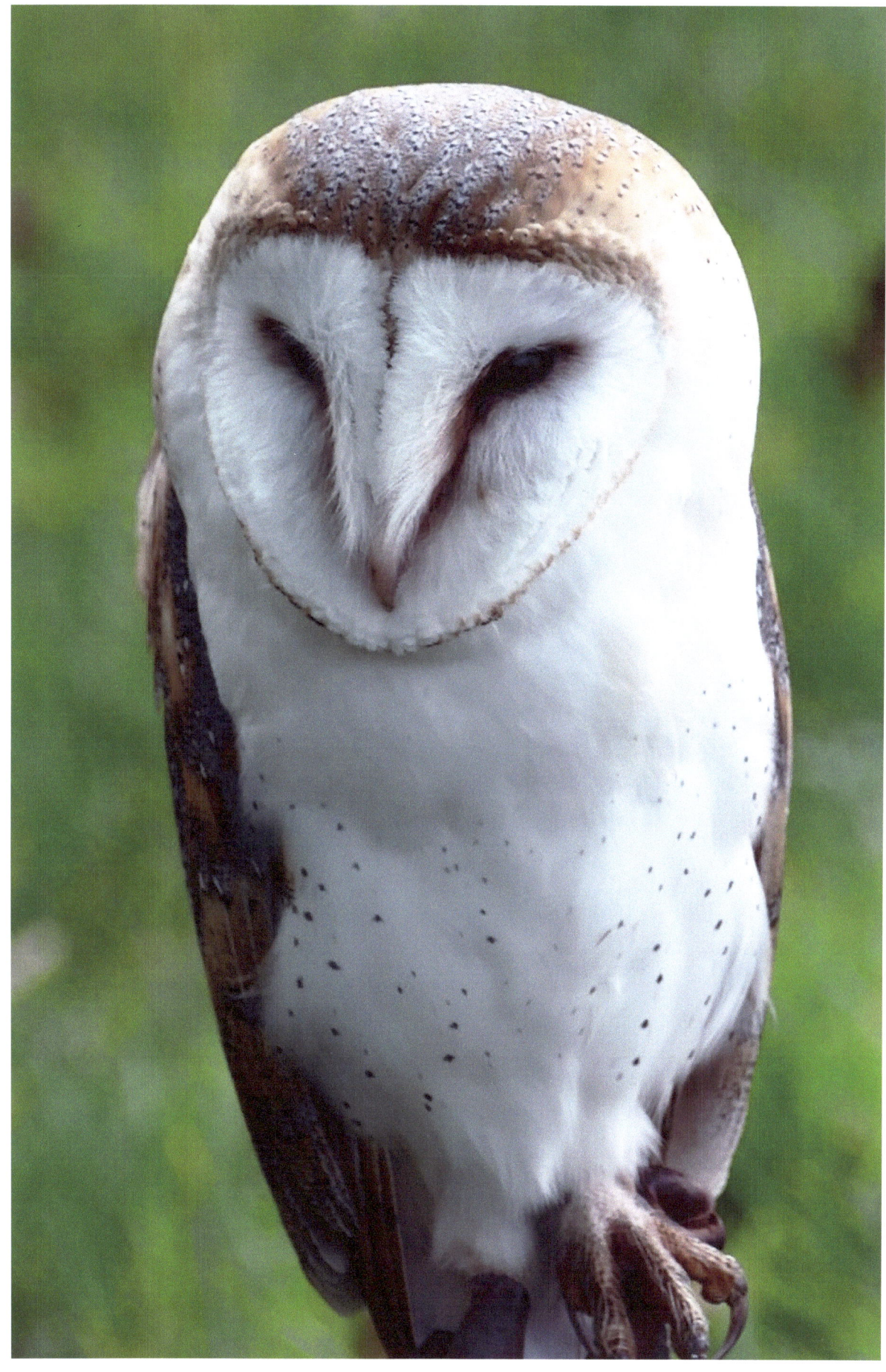

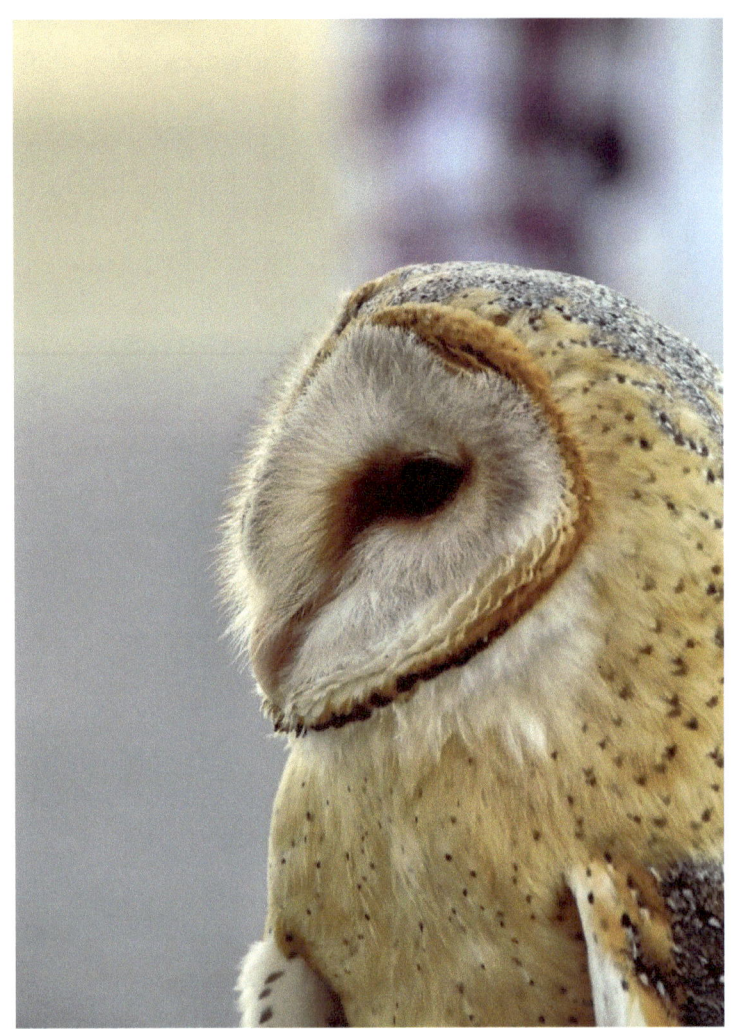
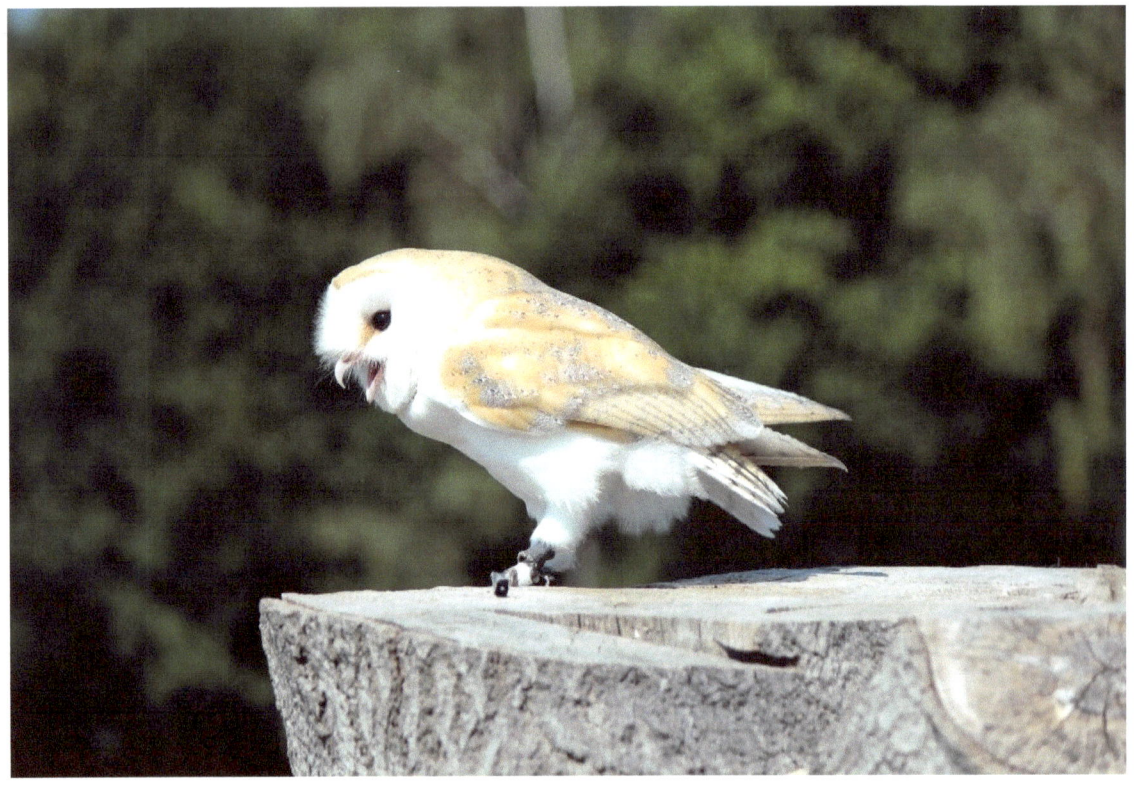

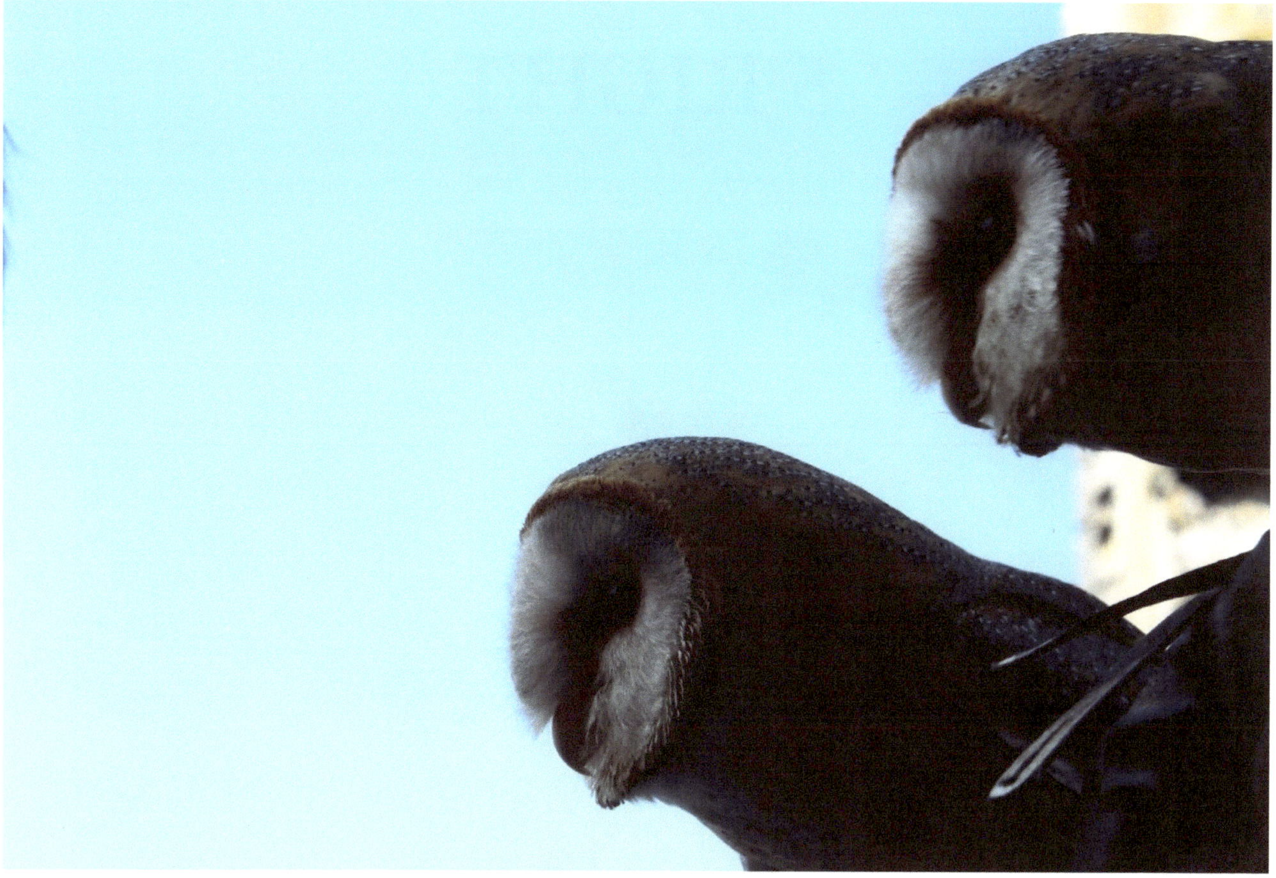

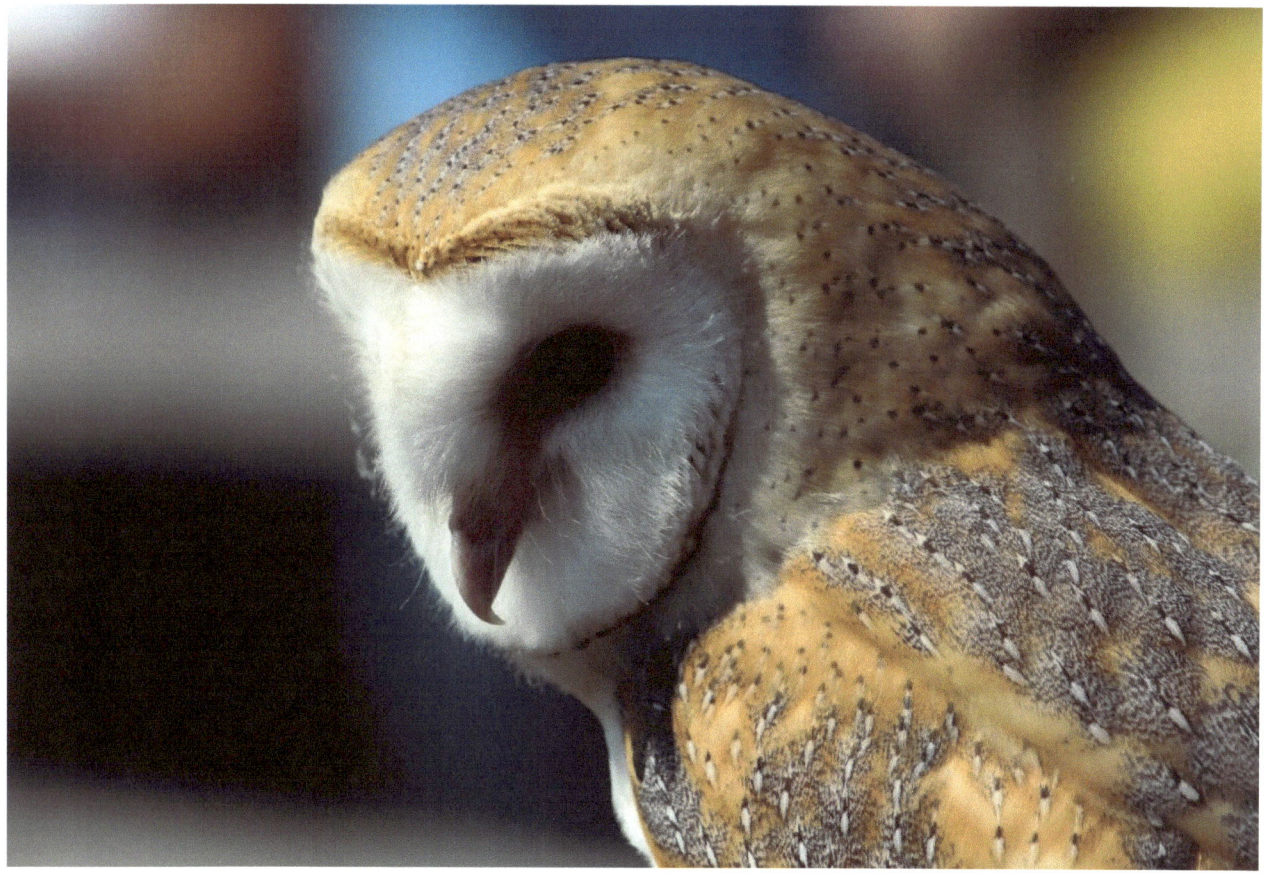

5 RIGHT

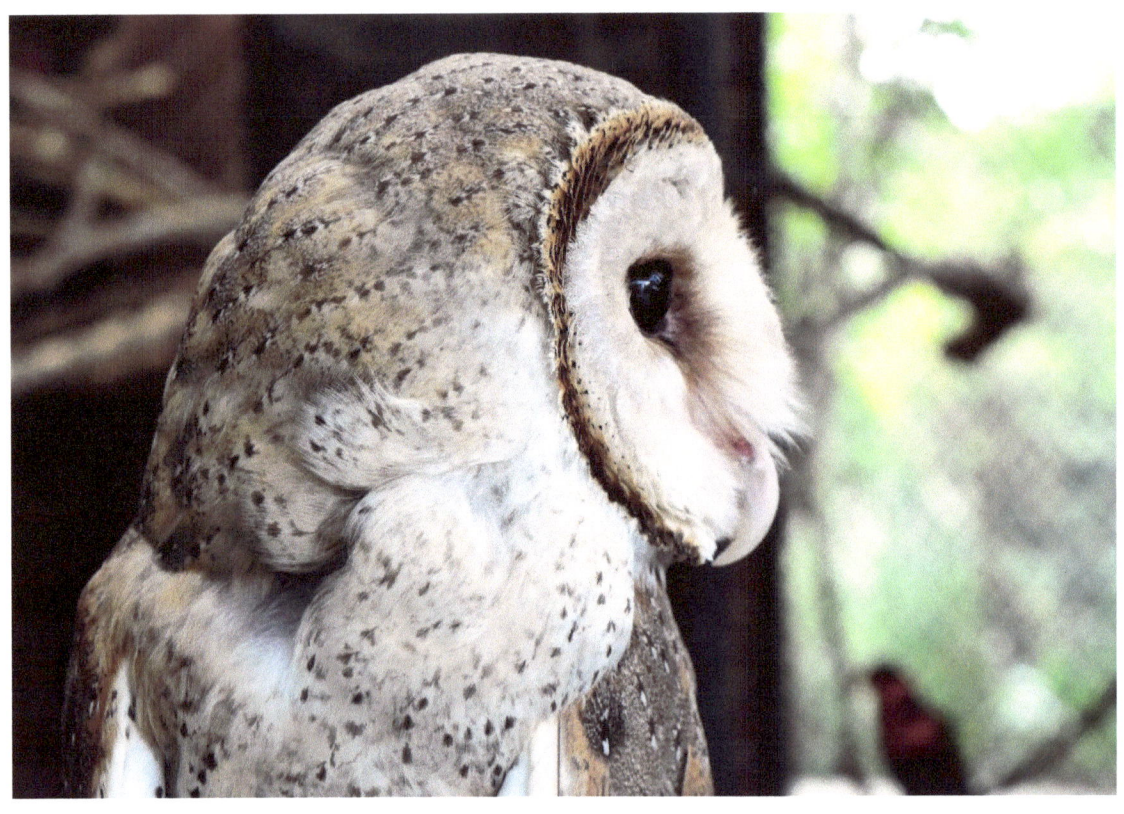

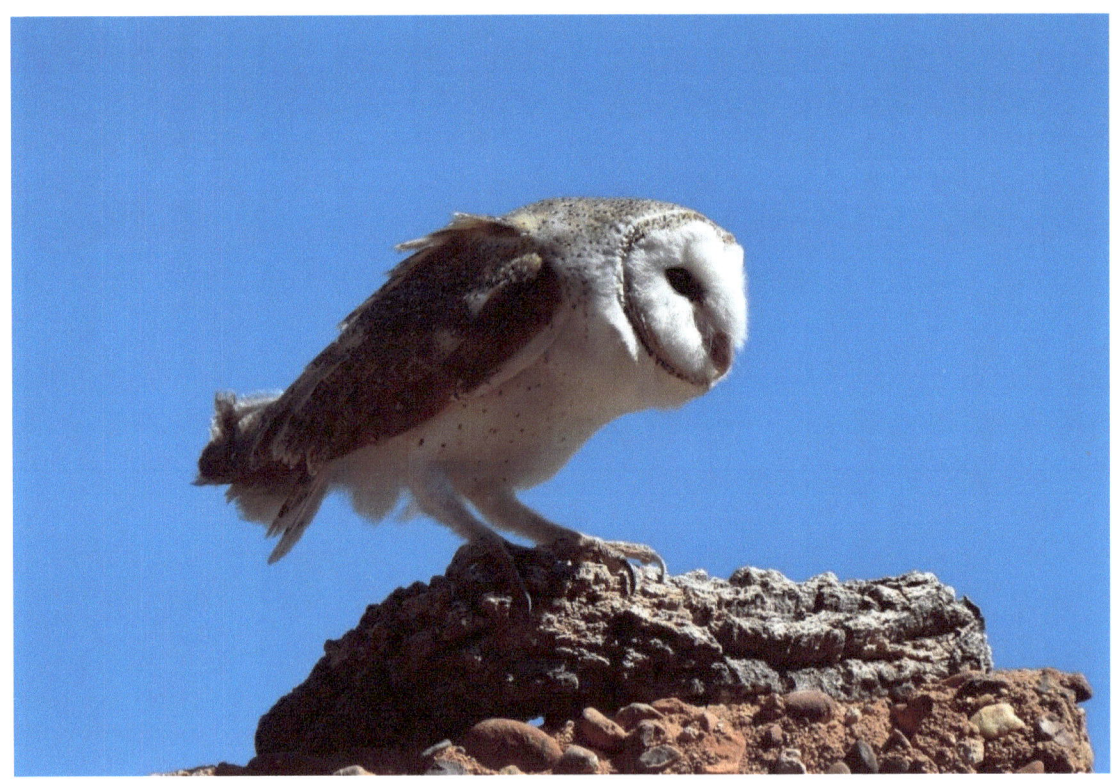

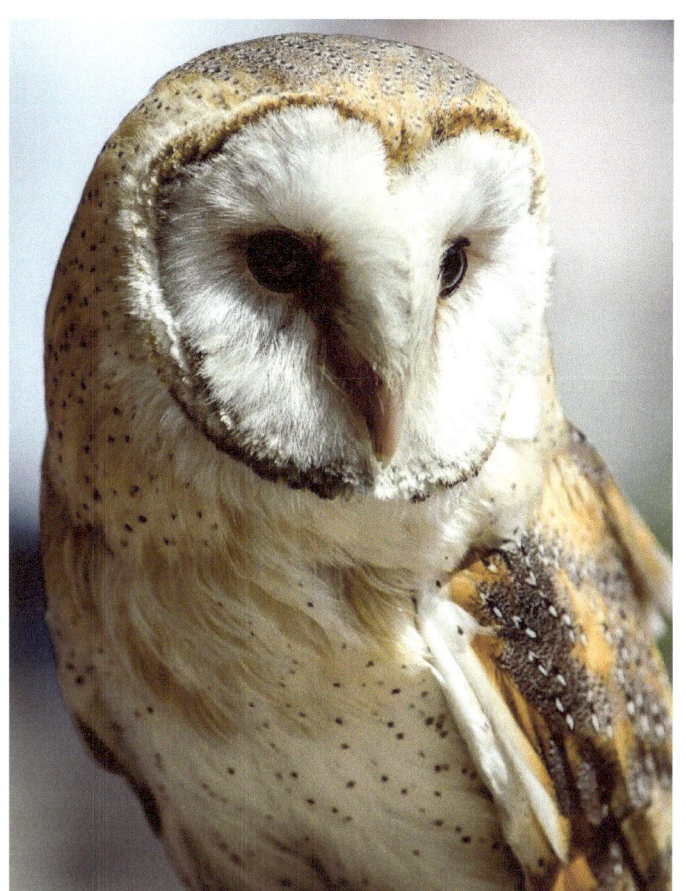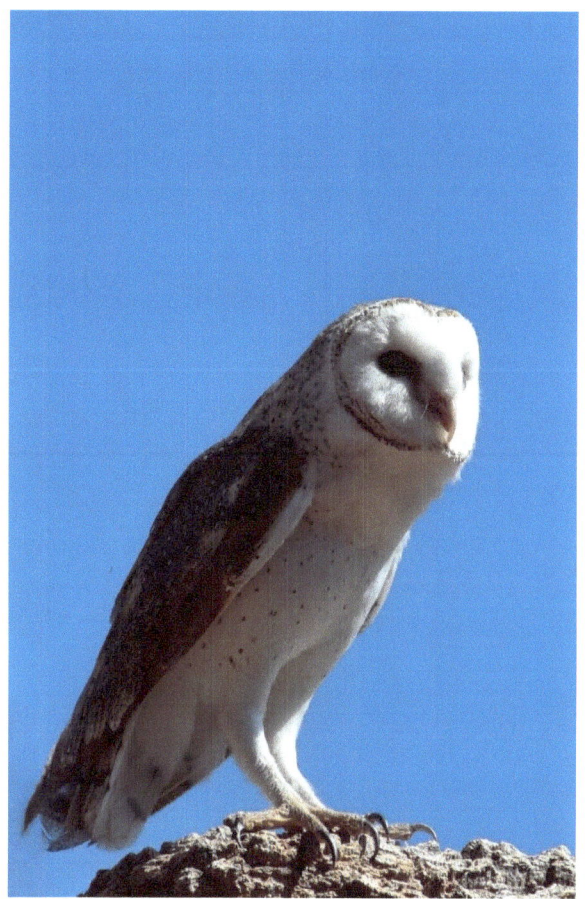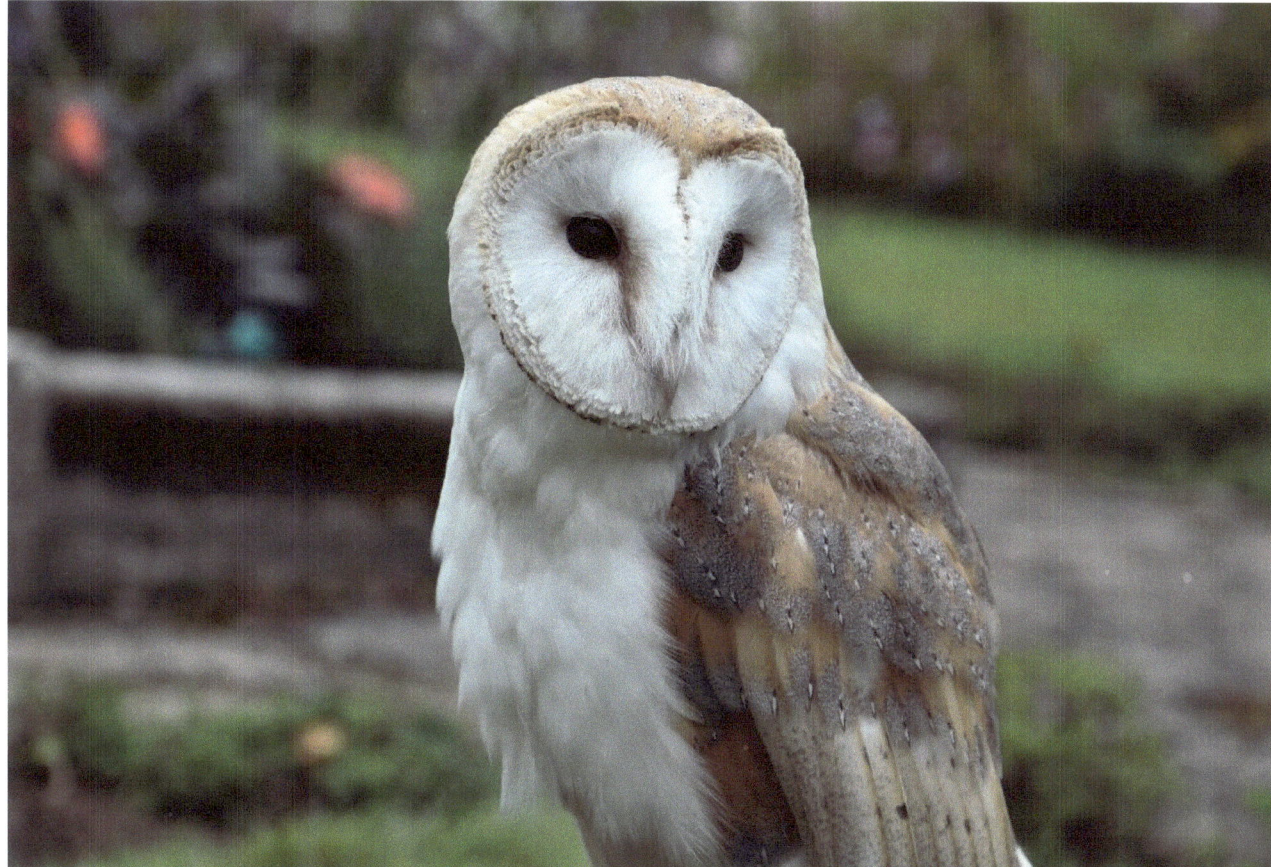

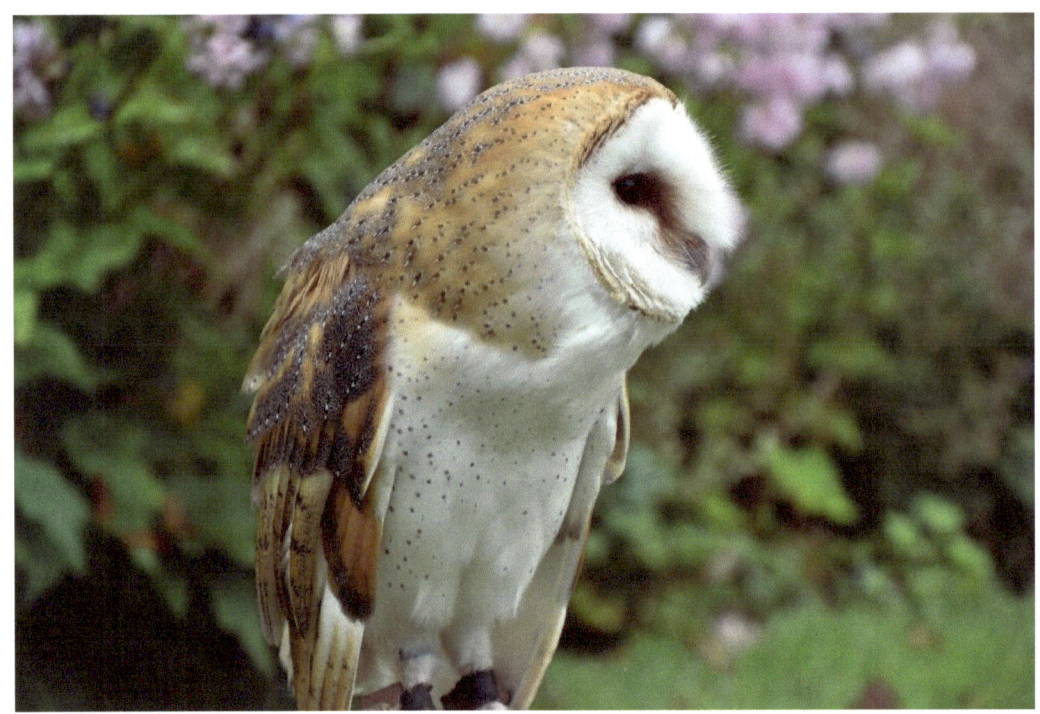
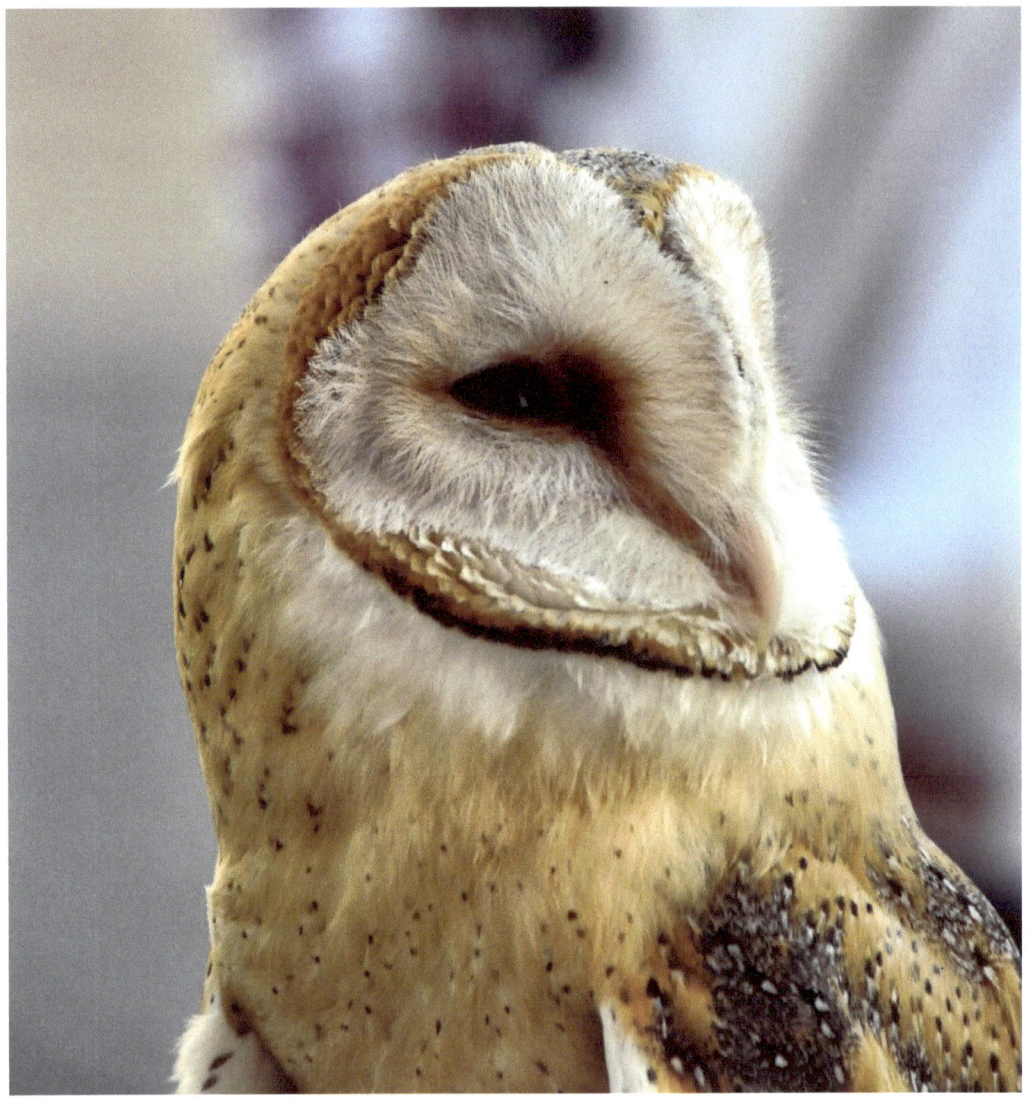

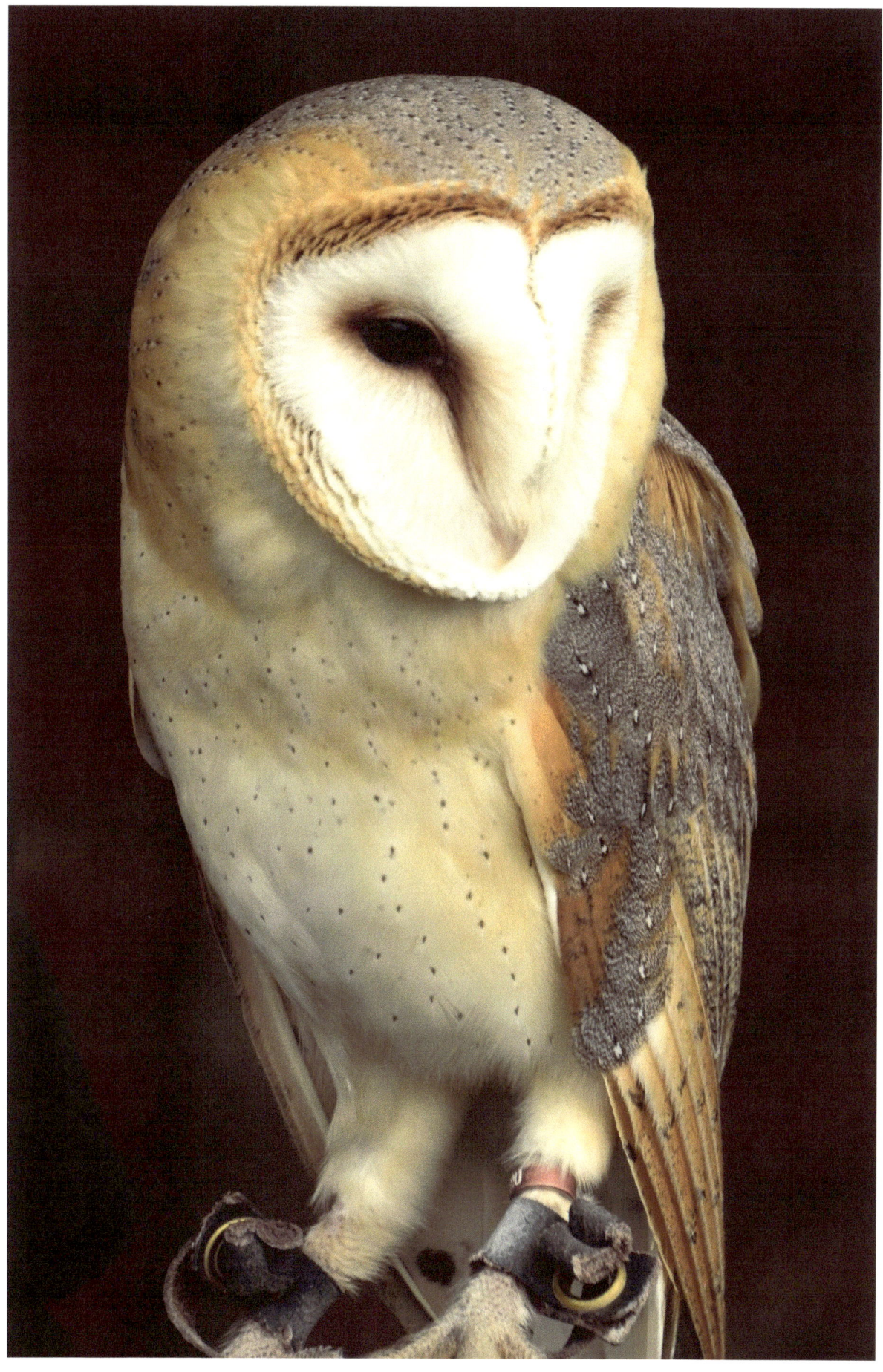

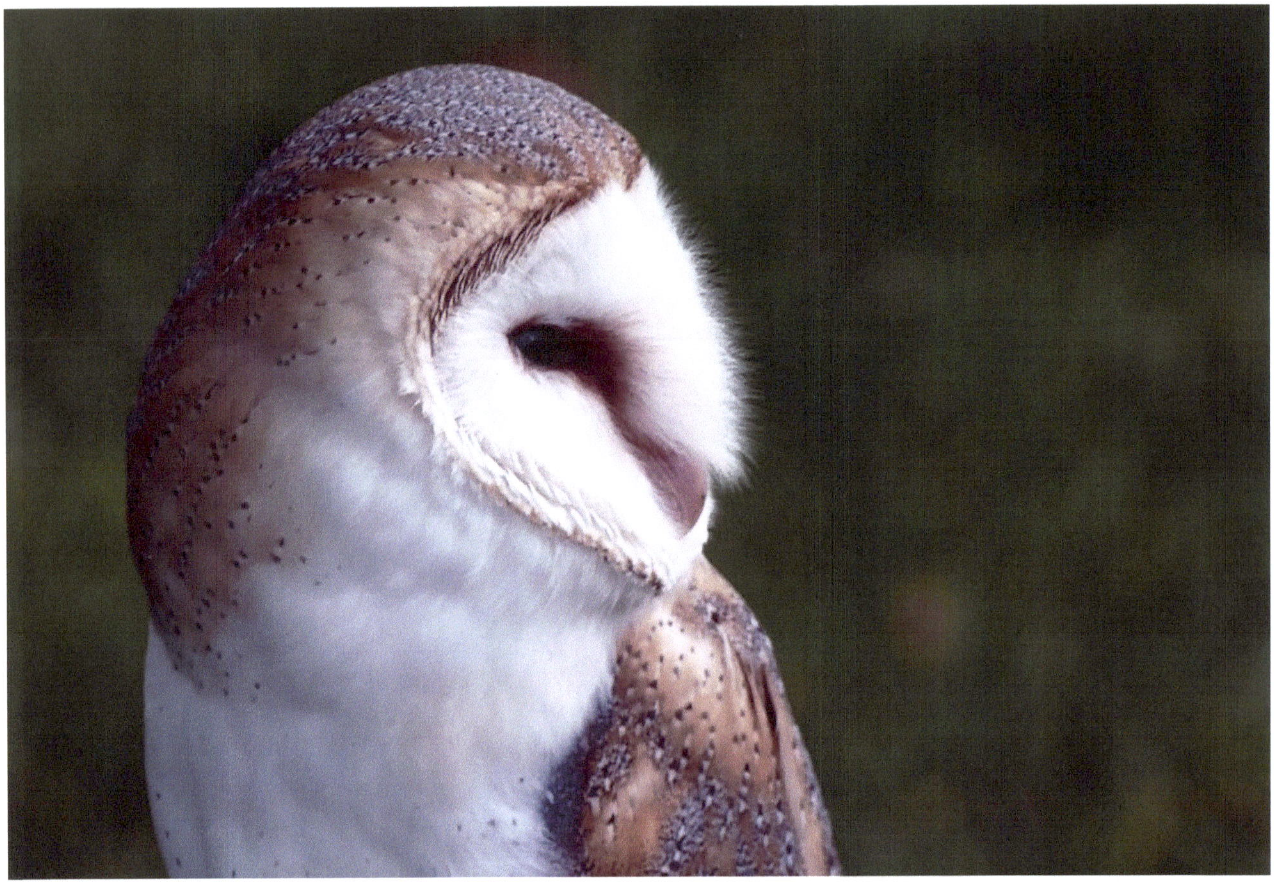

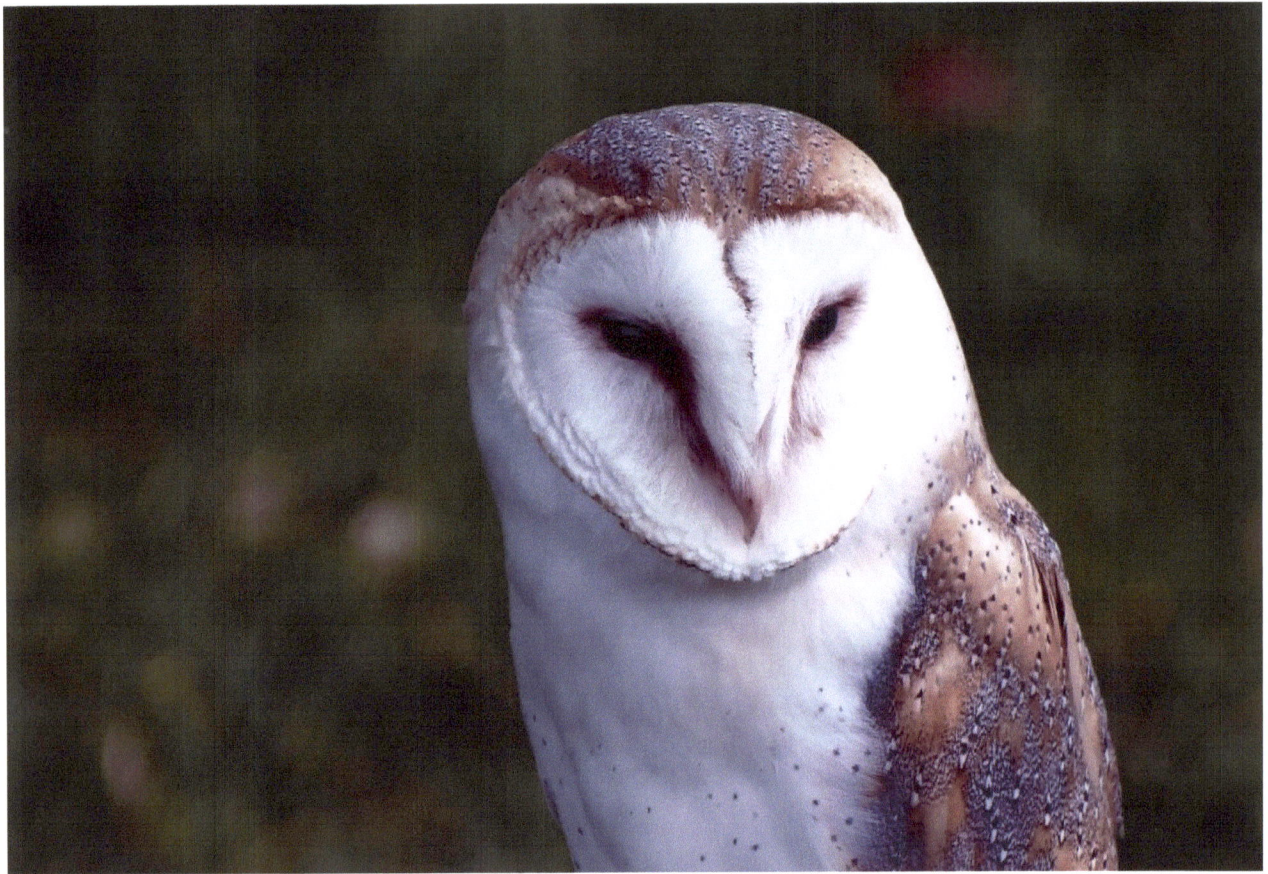

6 OWLNESS

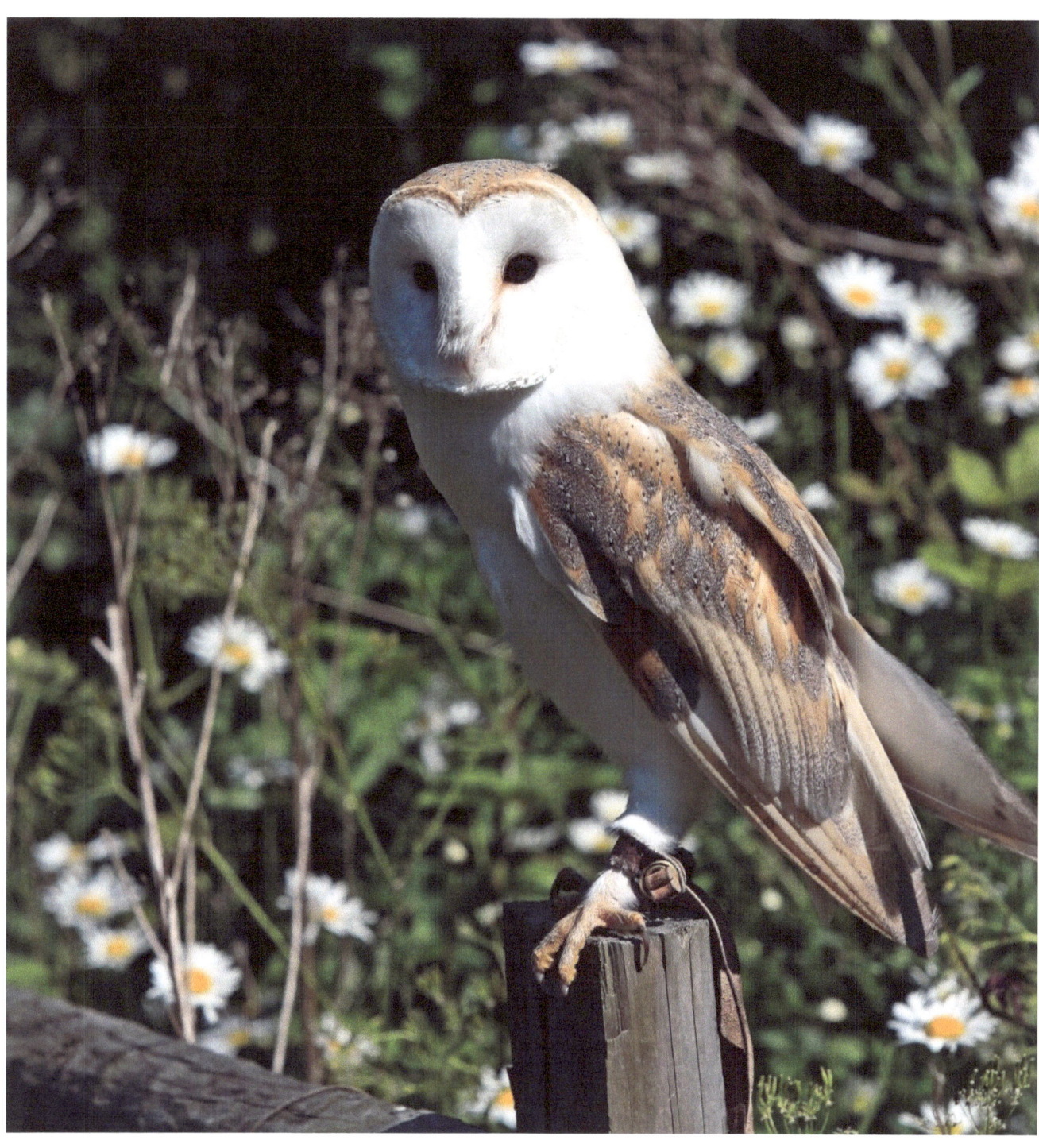

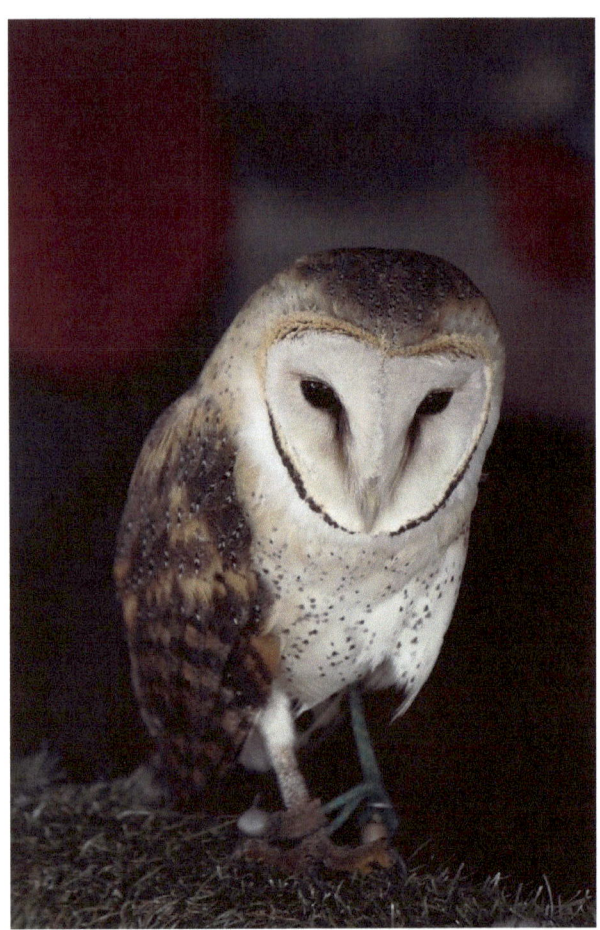
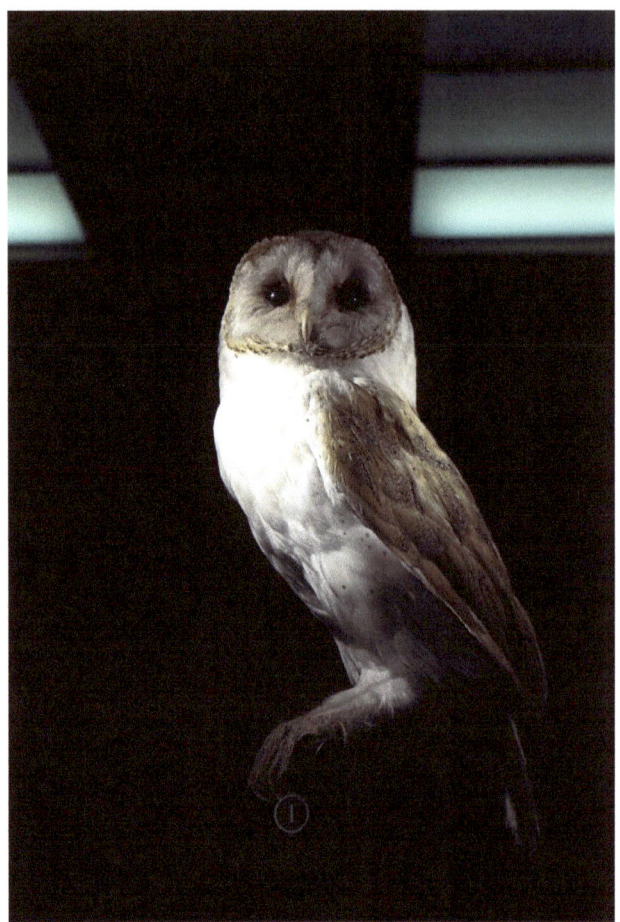
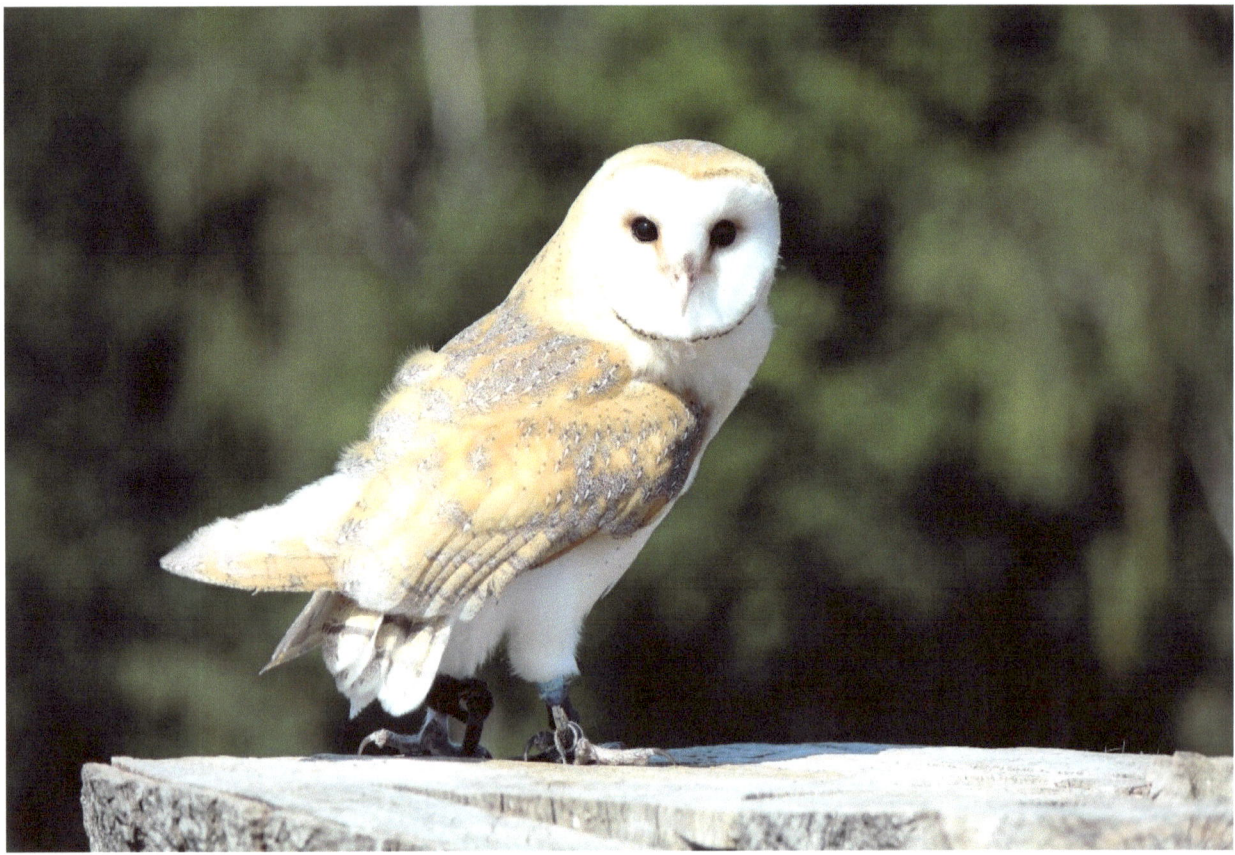

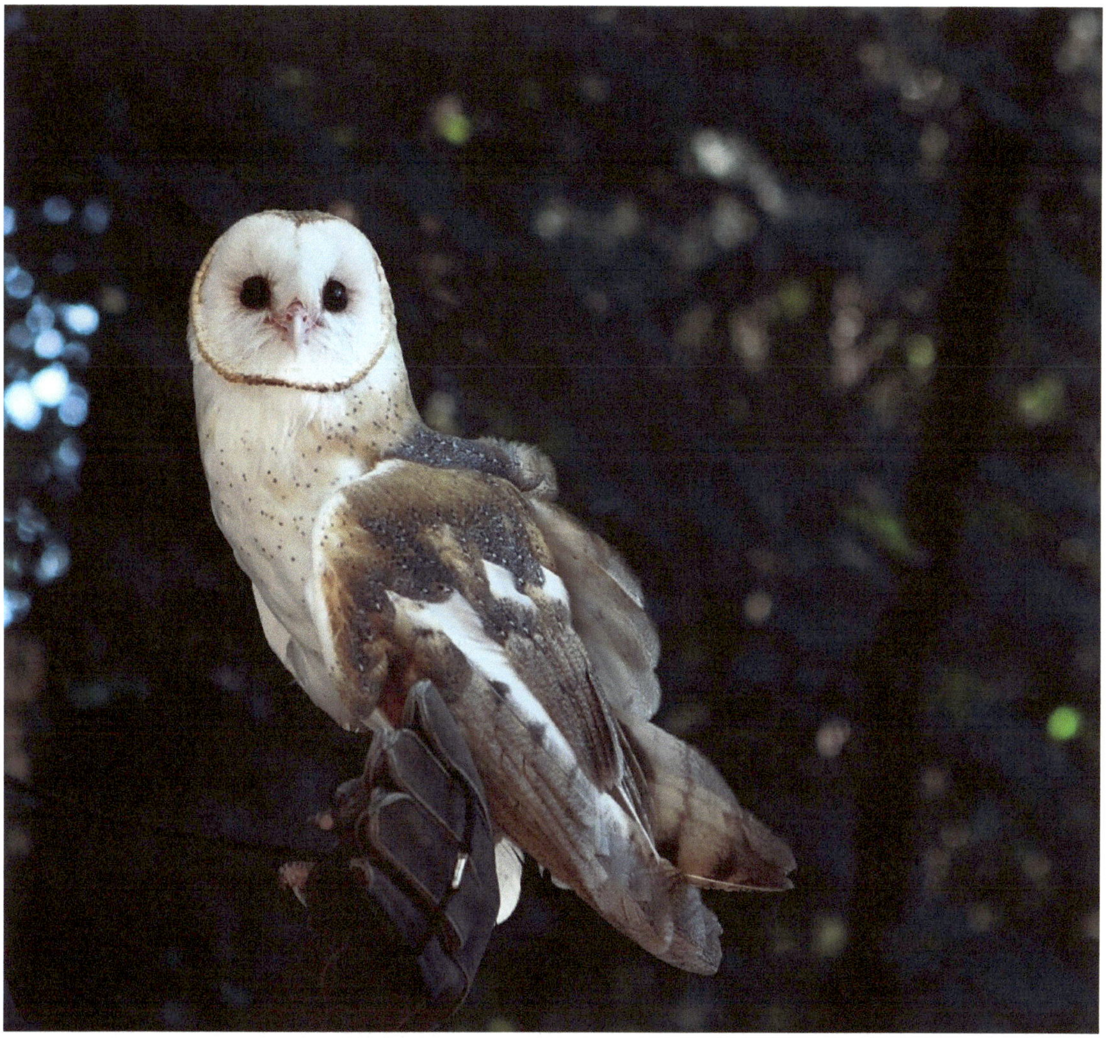

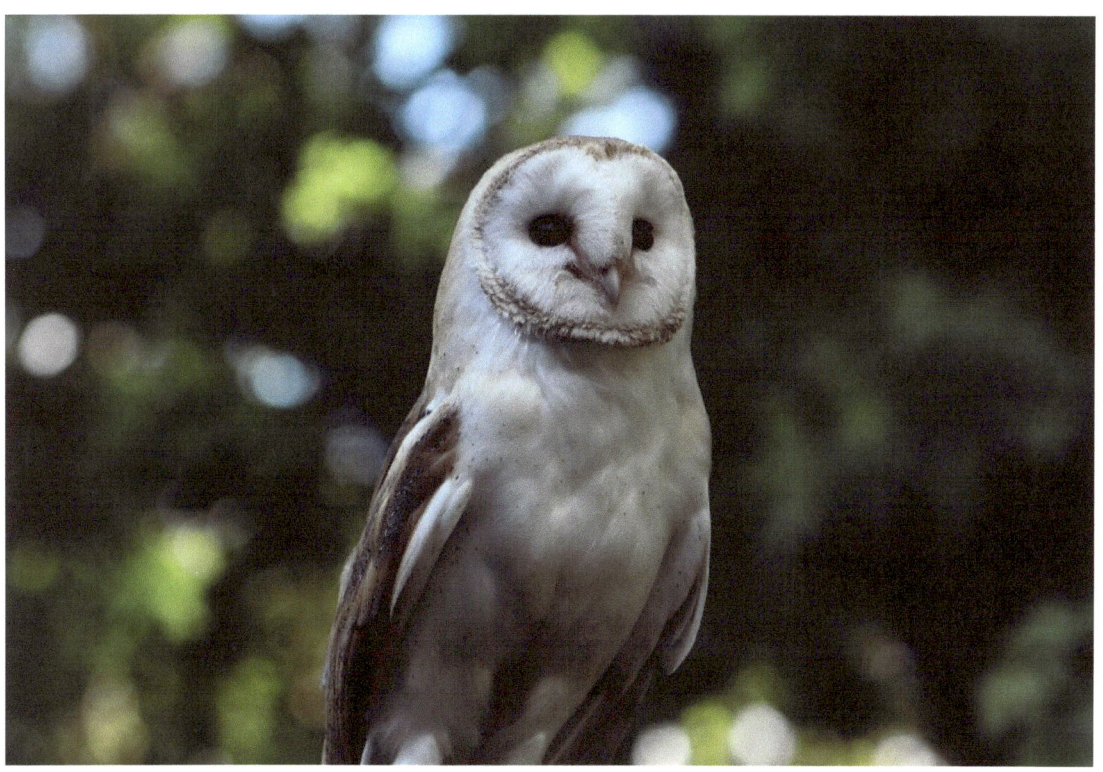

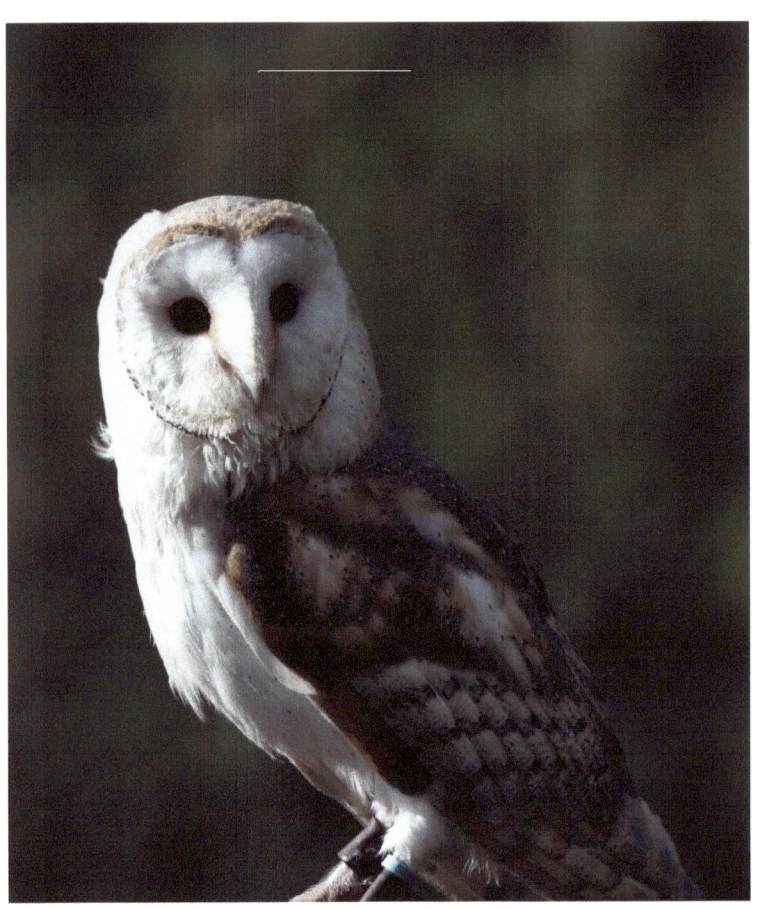
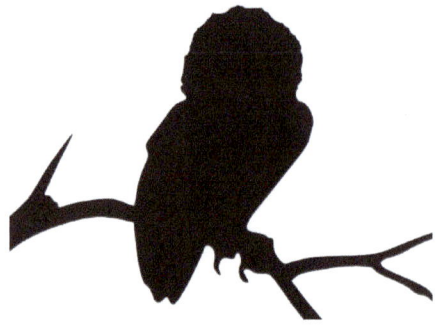

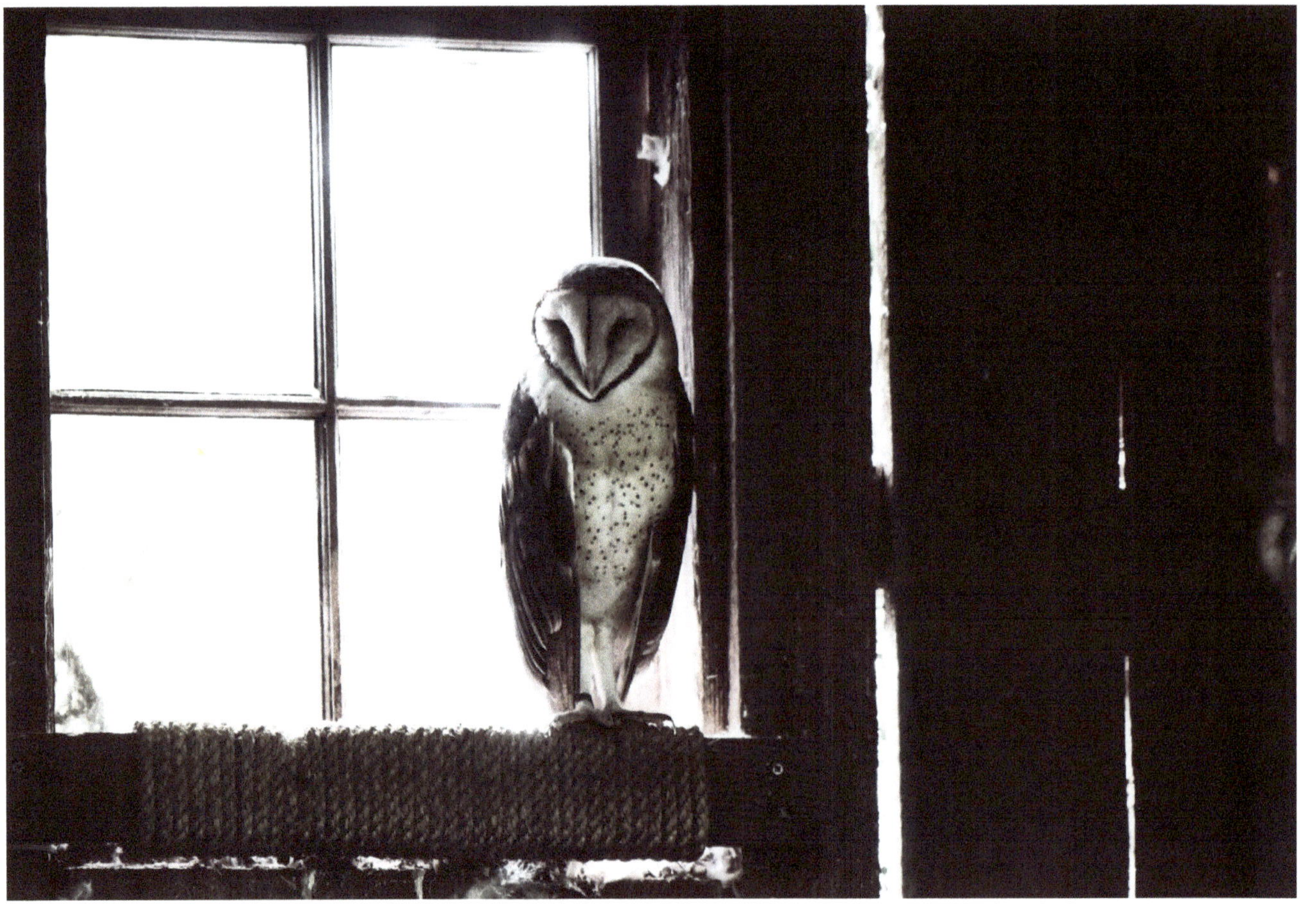

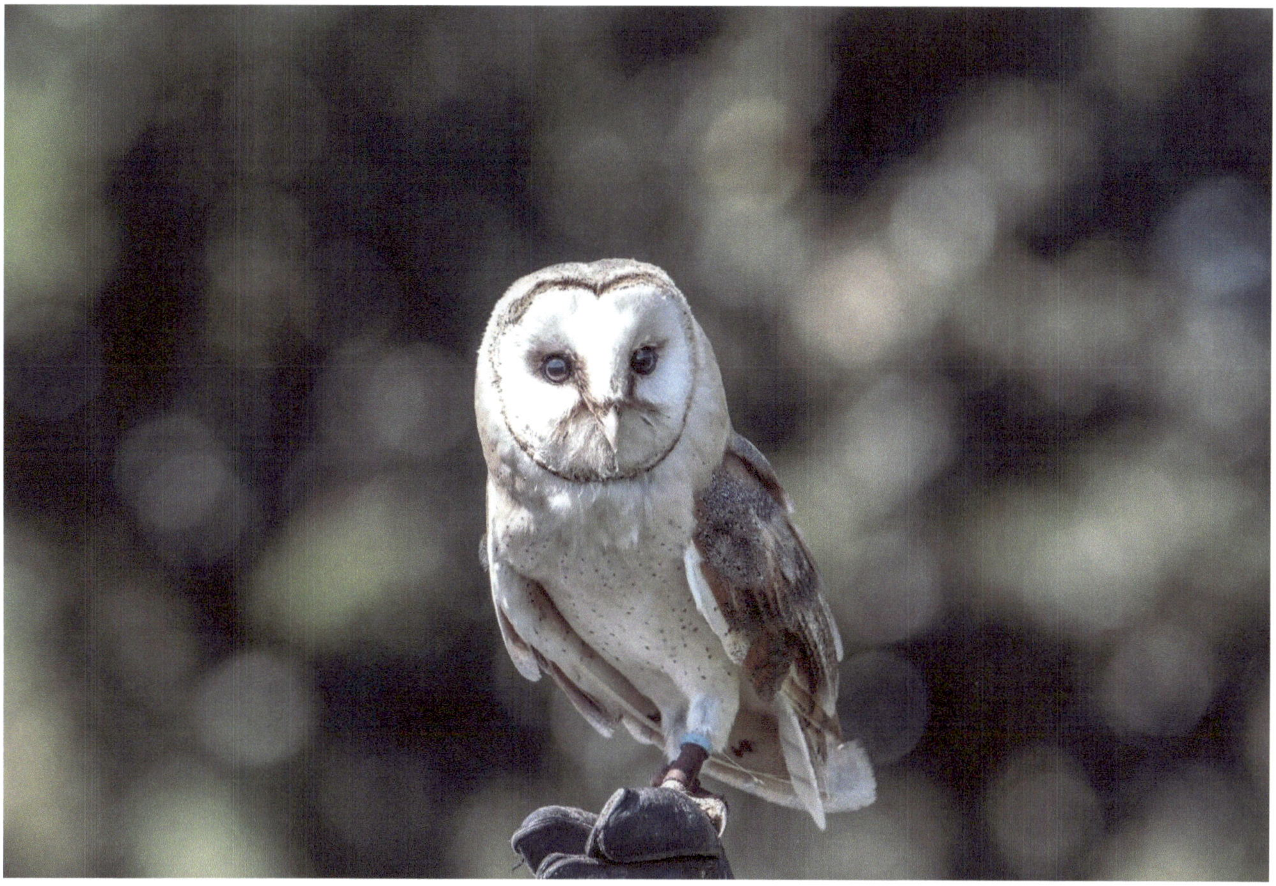

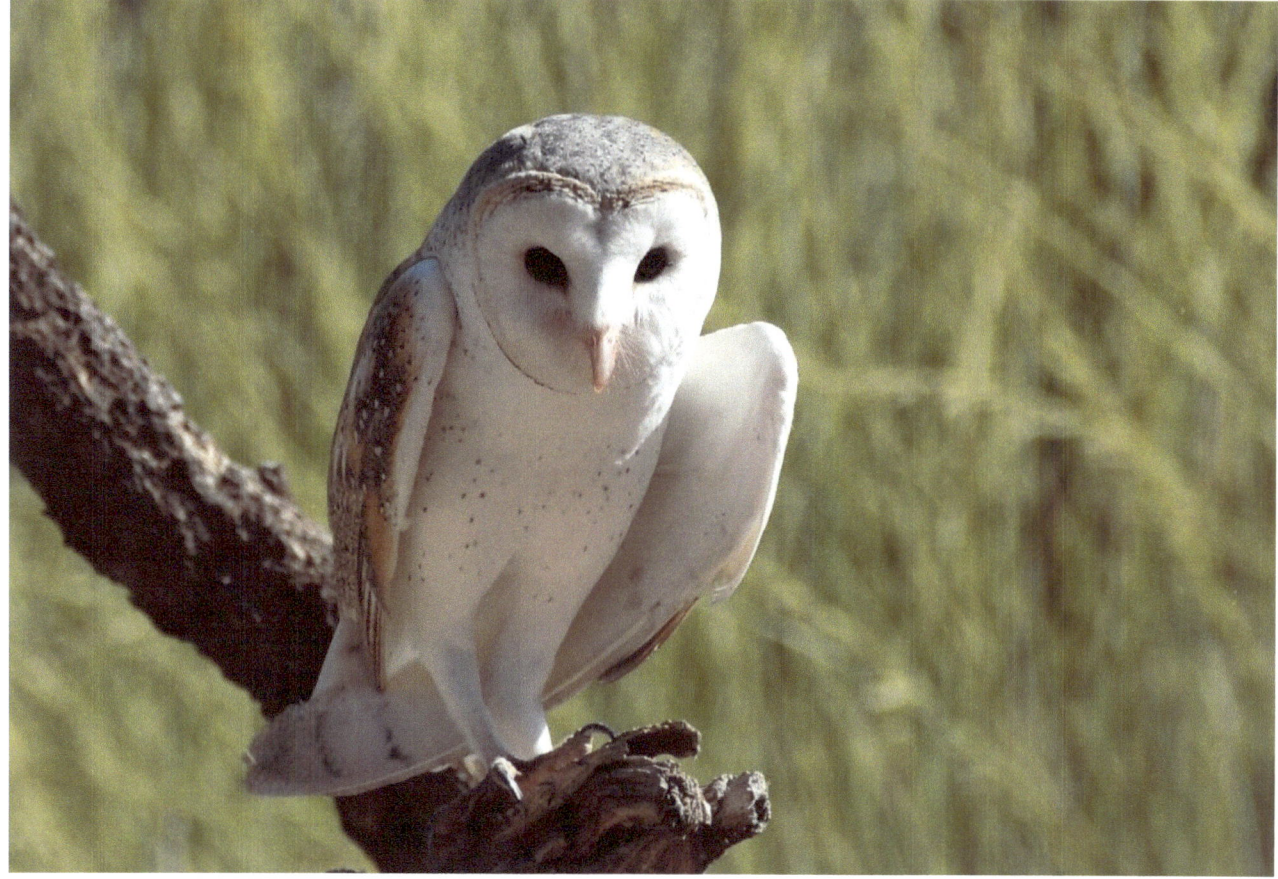

7 COLOR

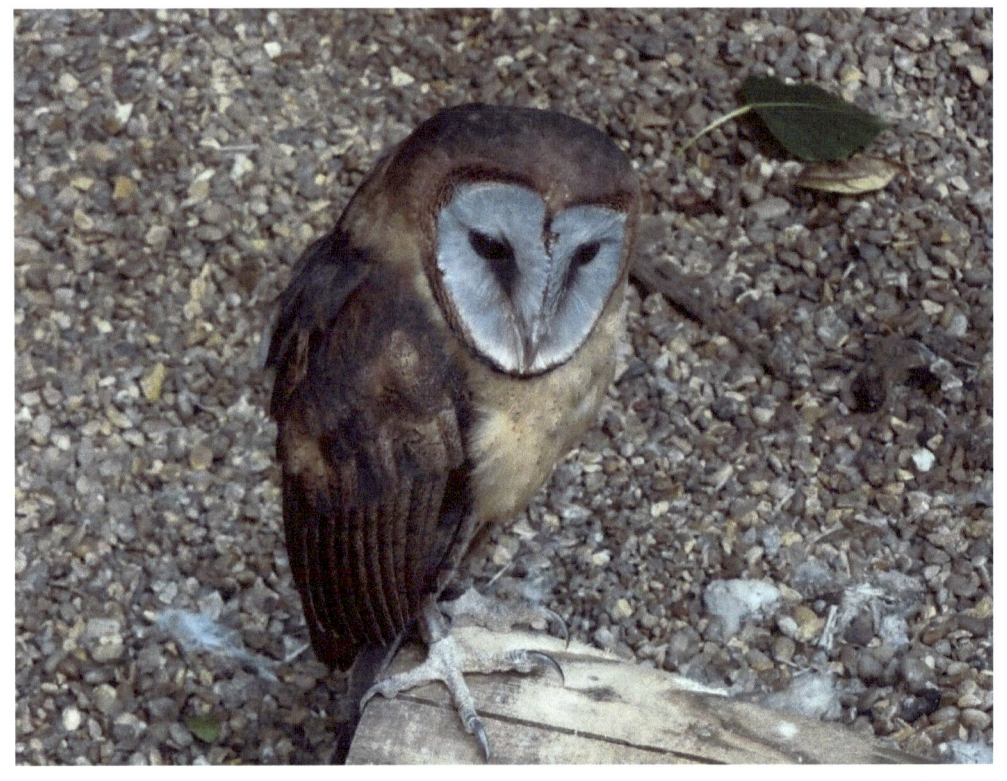

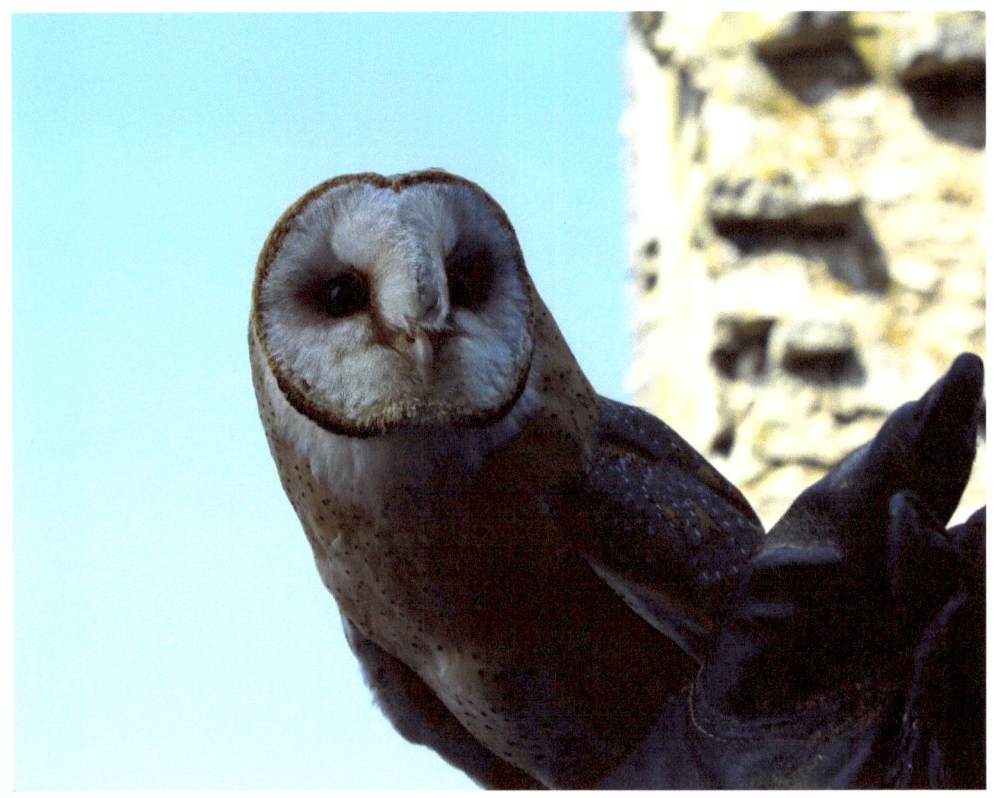

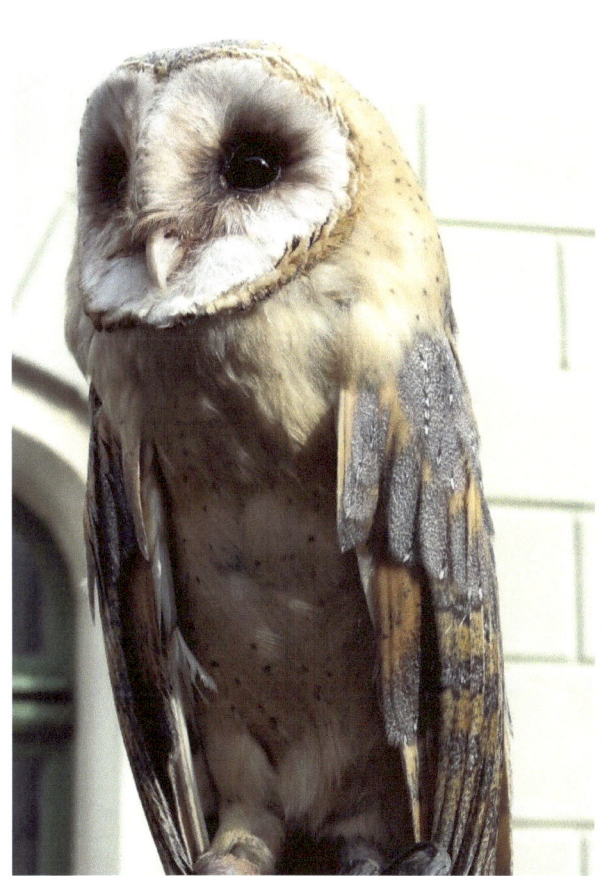
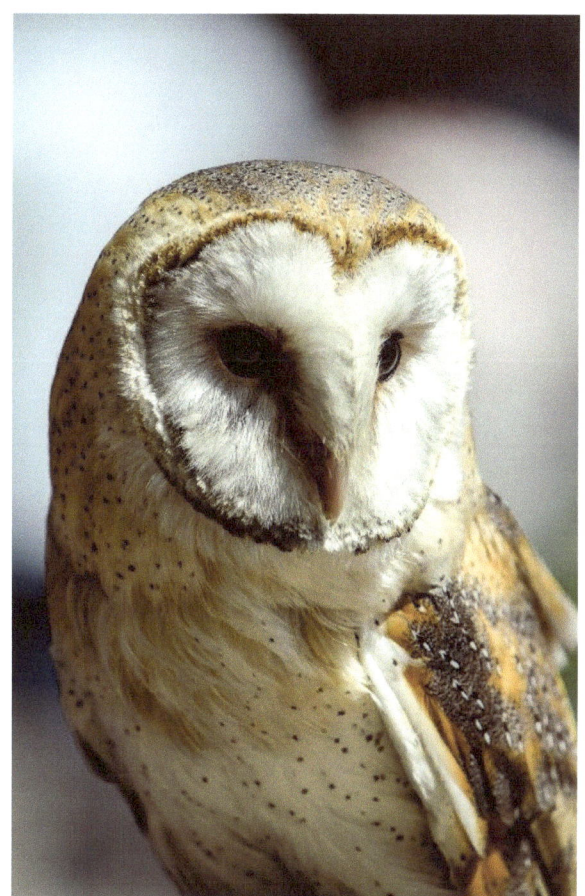
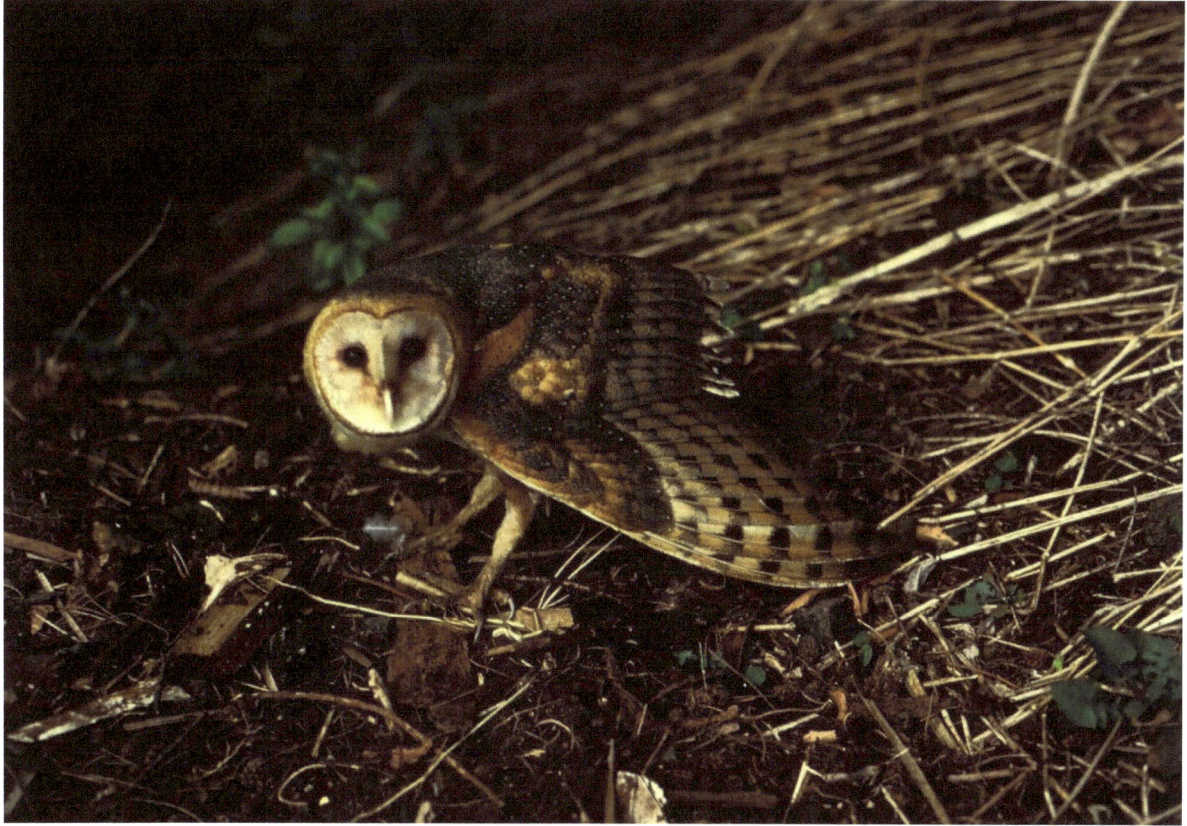

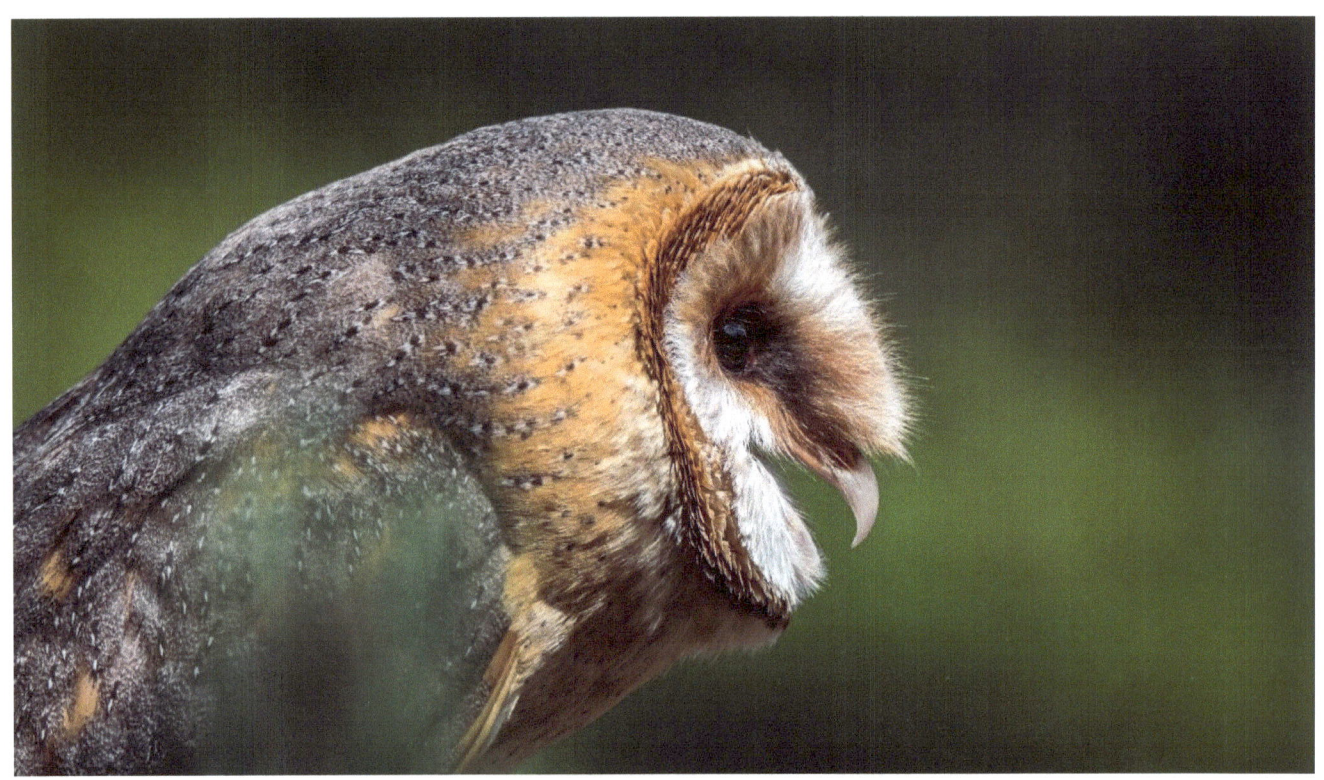
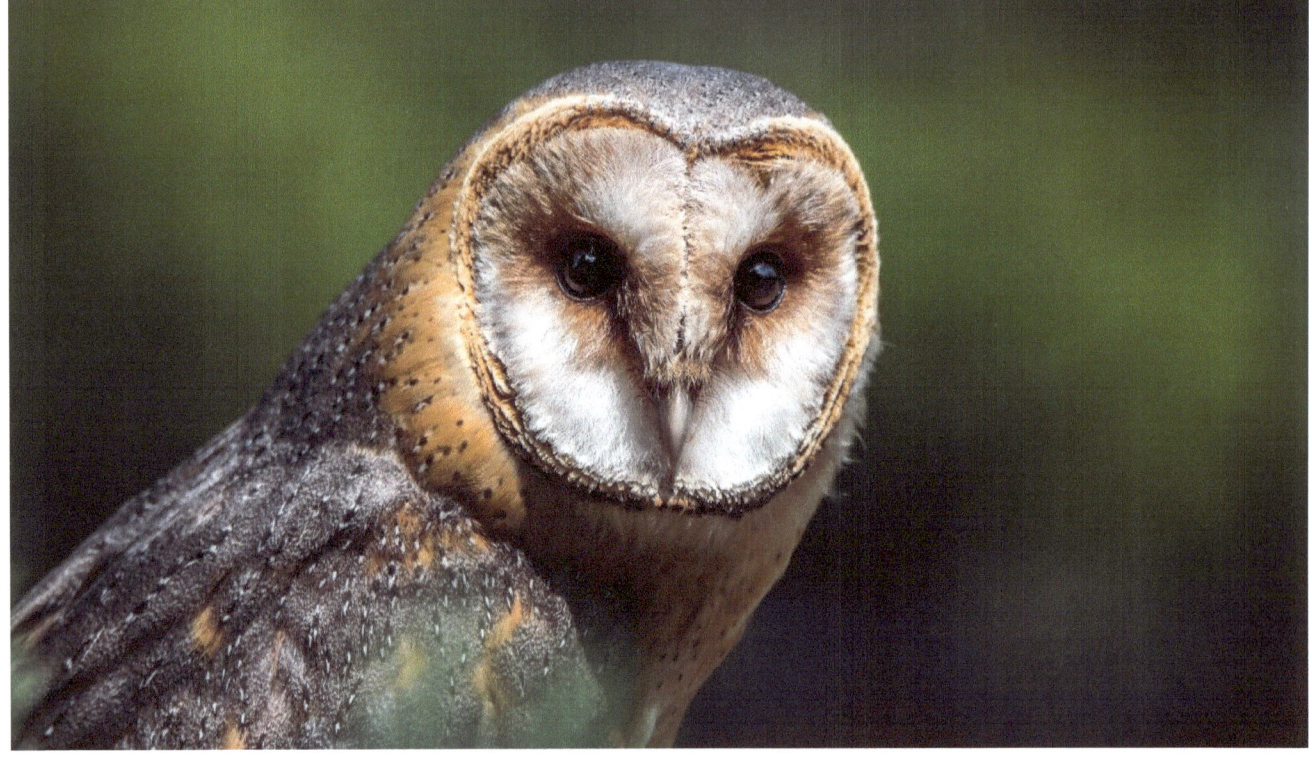
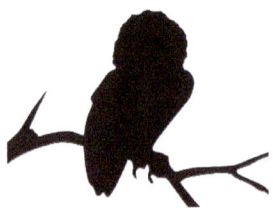

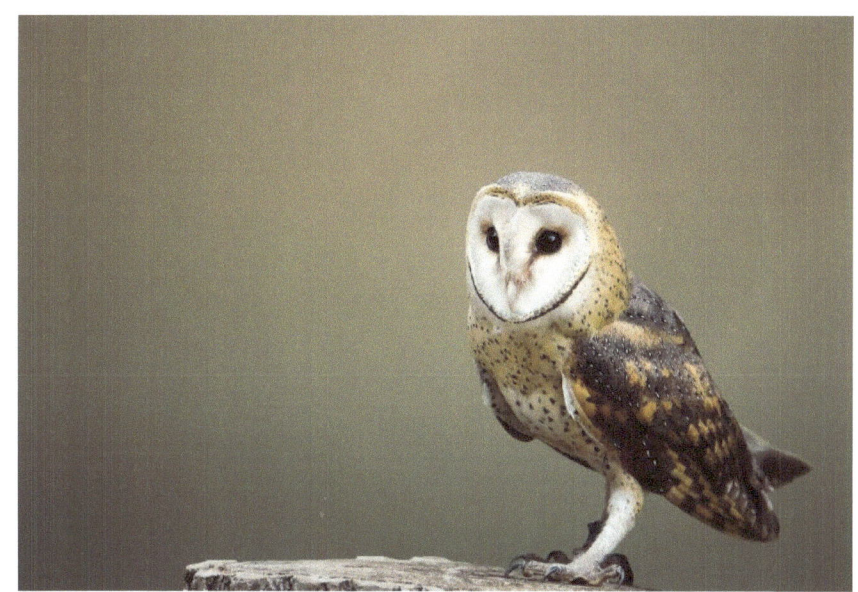
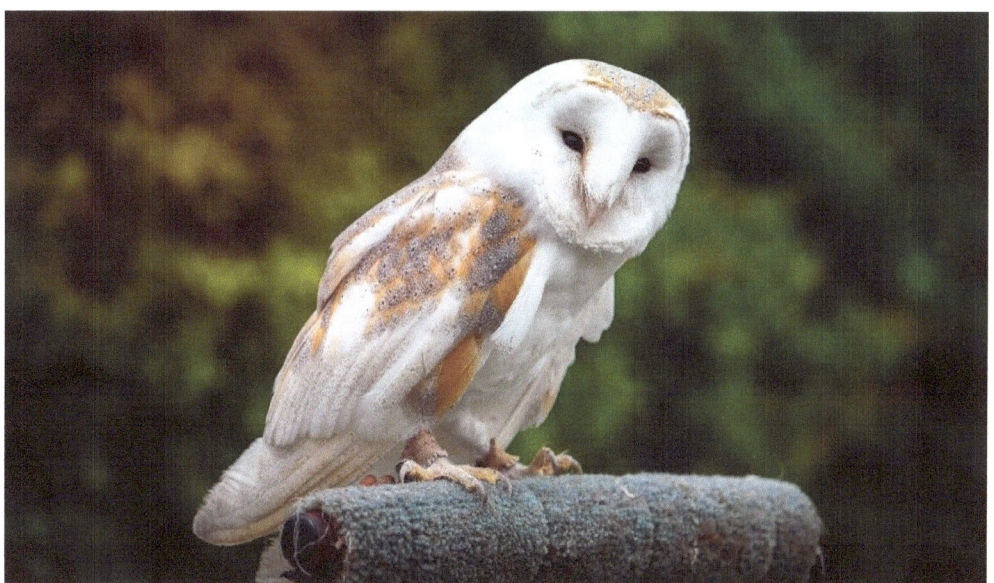
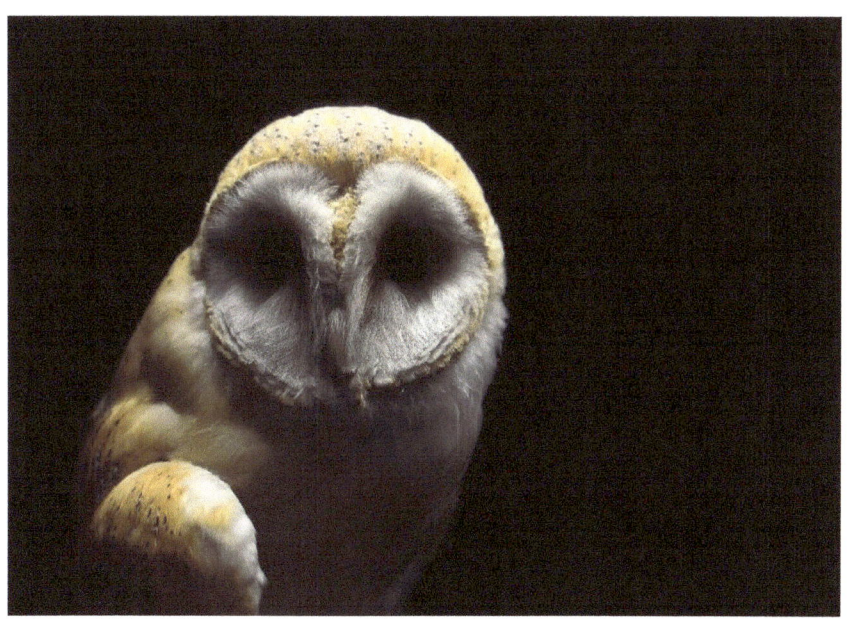

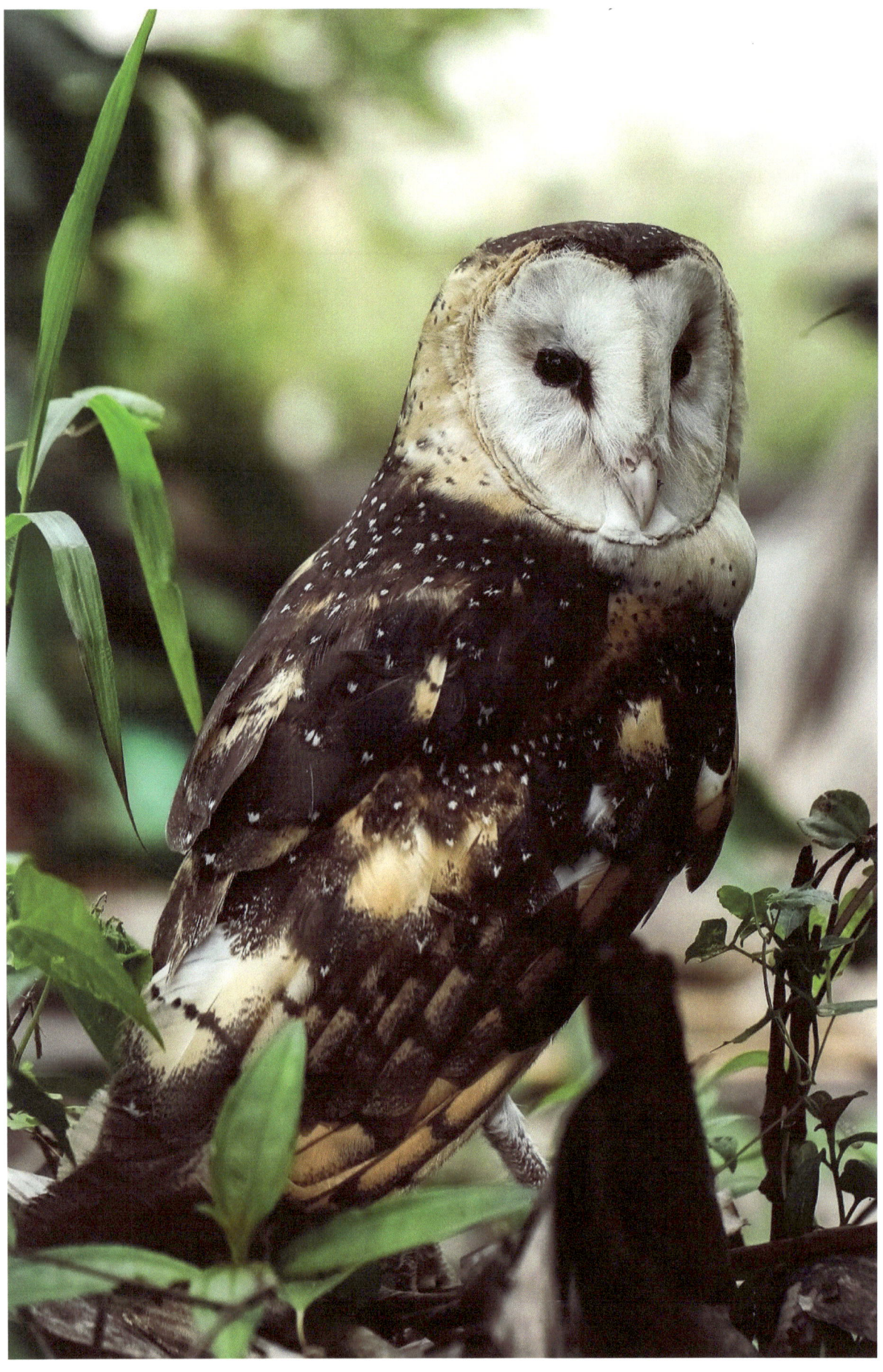

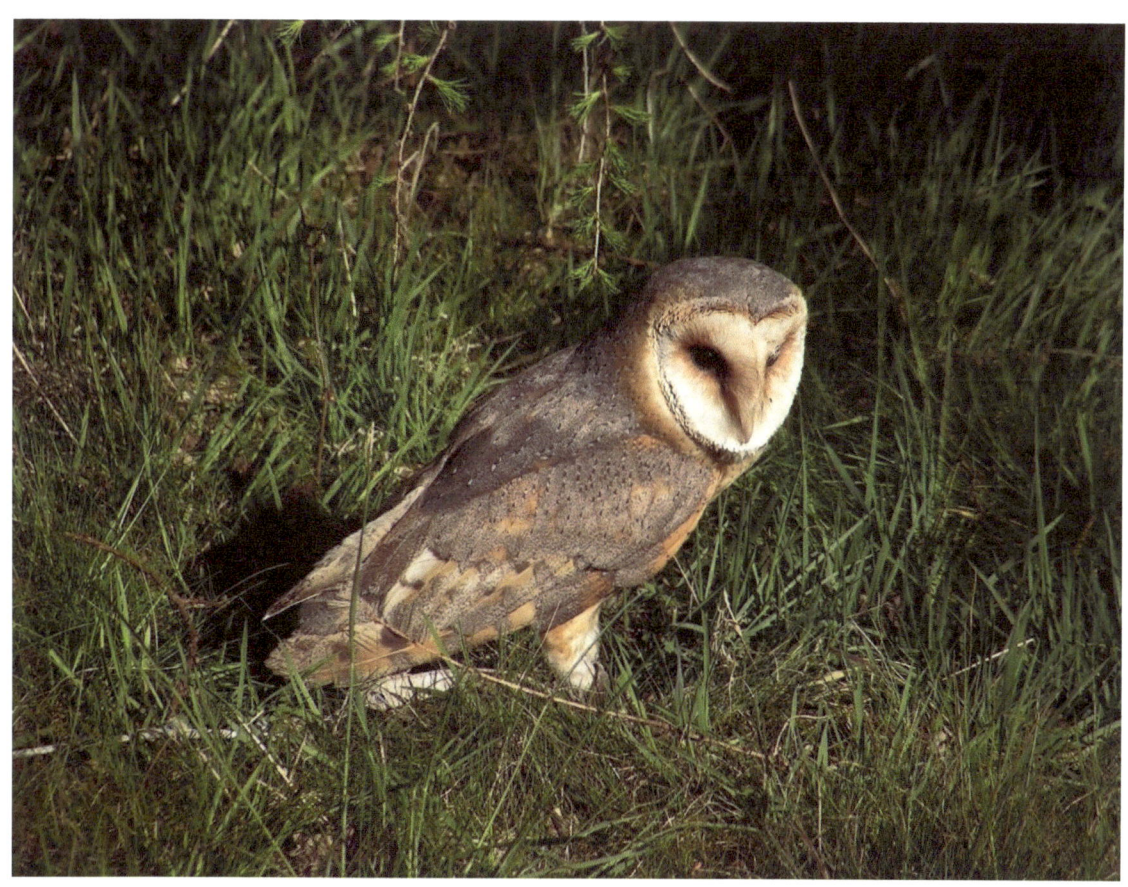
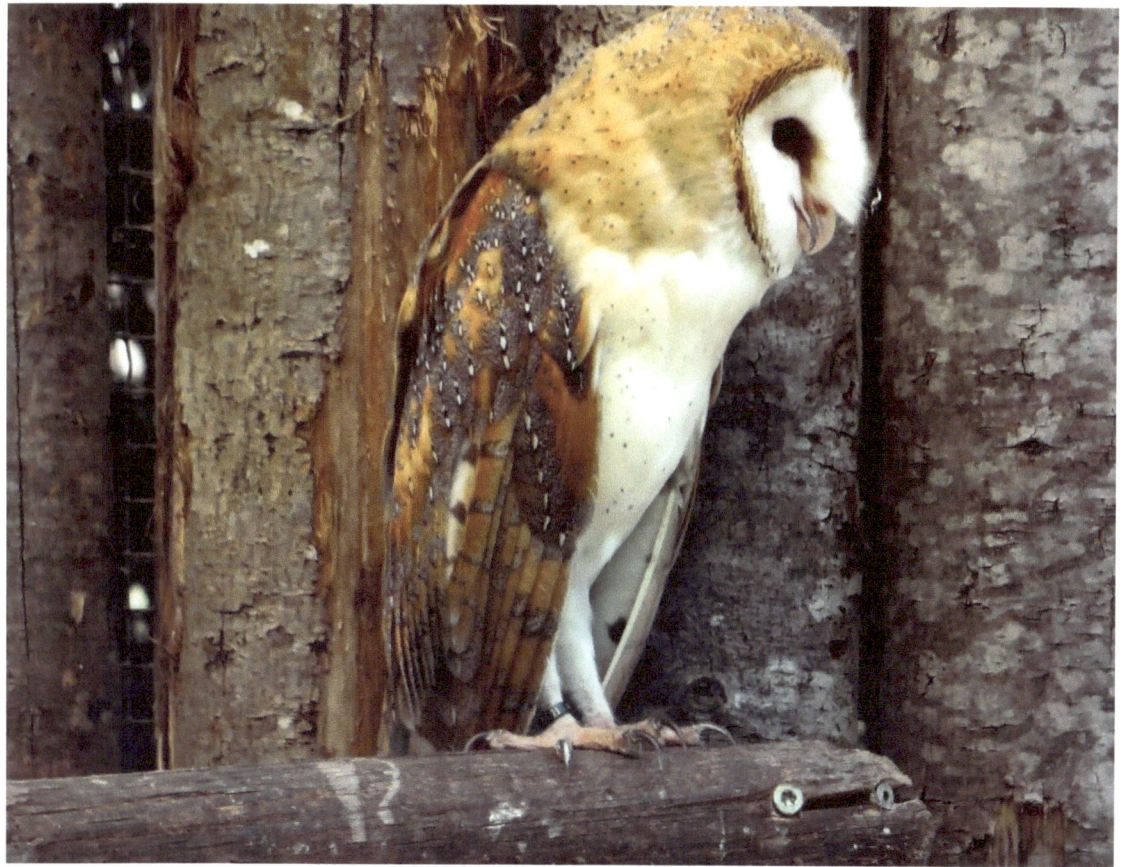

8 TALONS

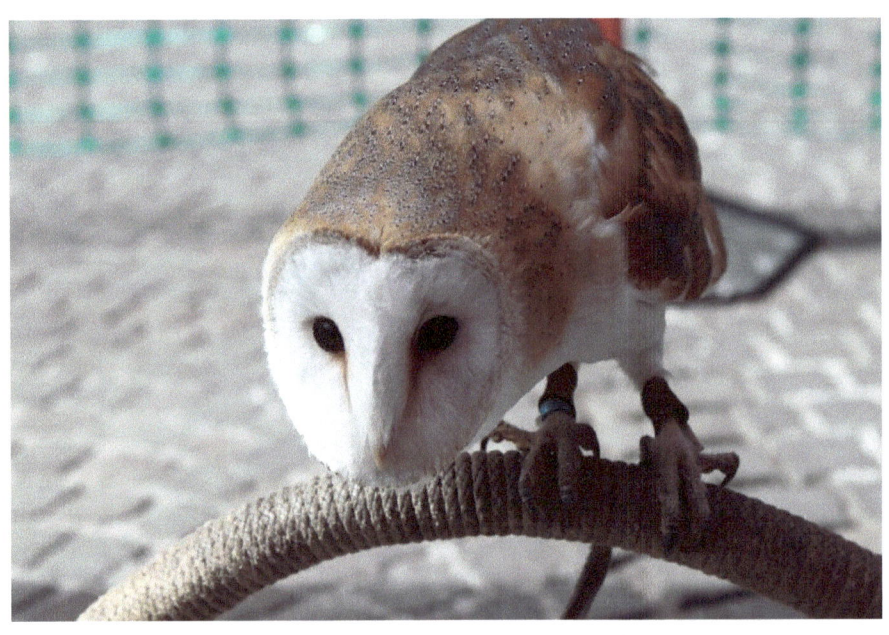

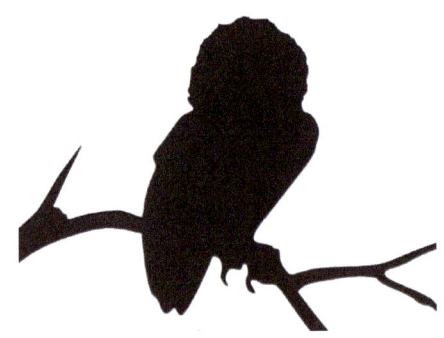

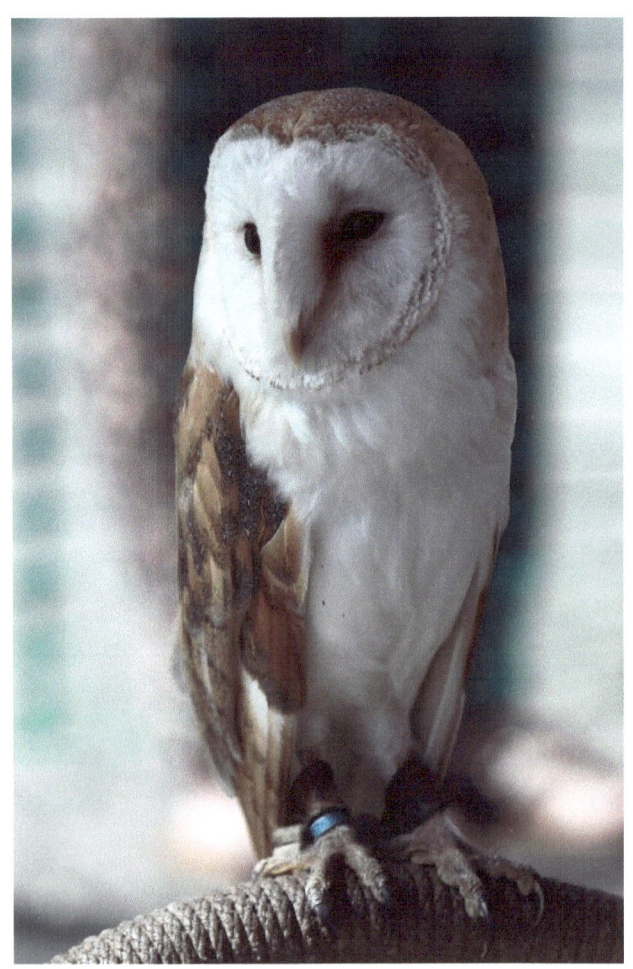

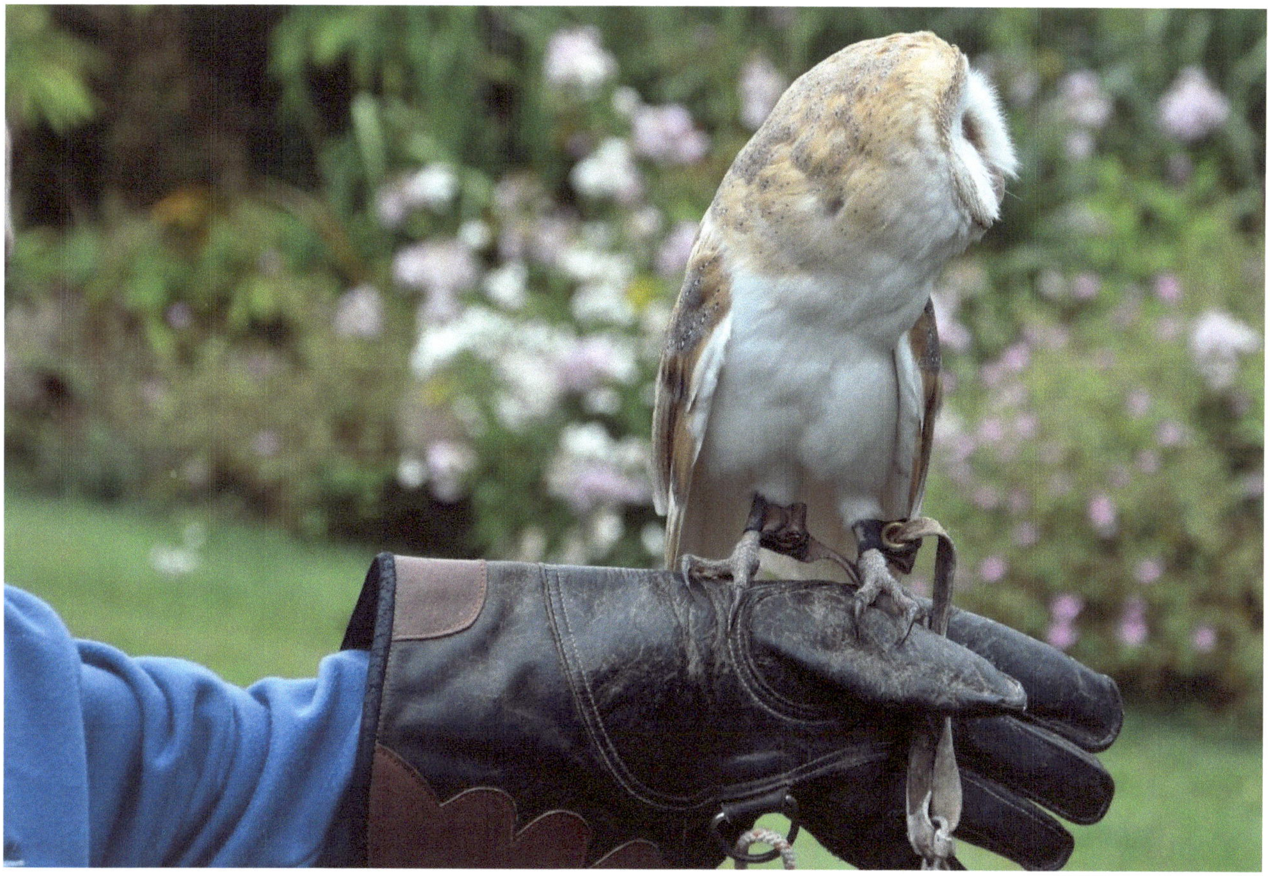

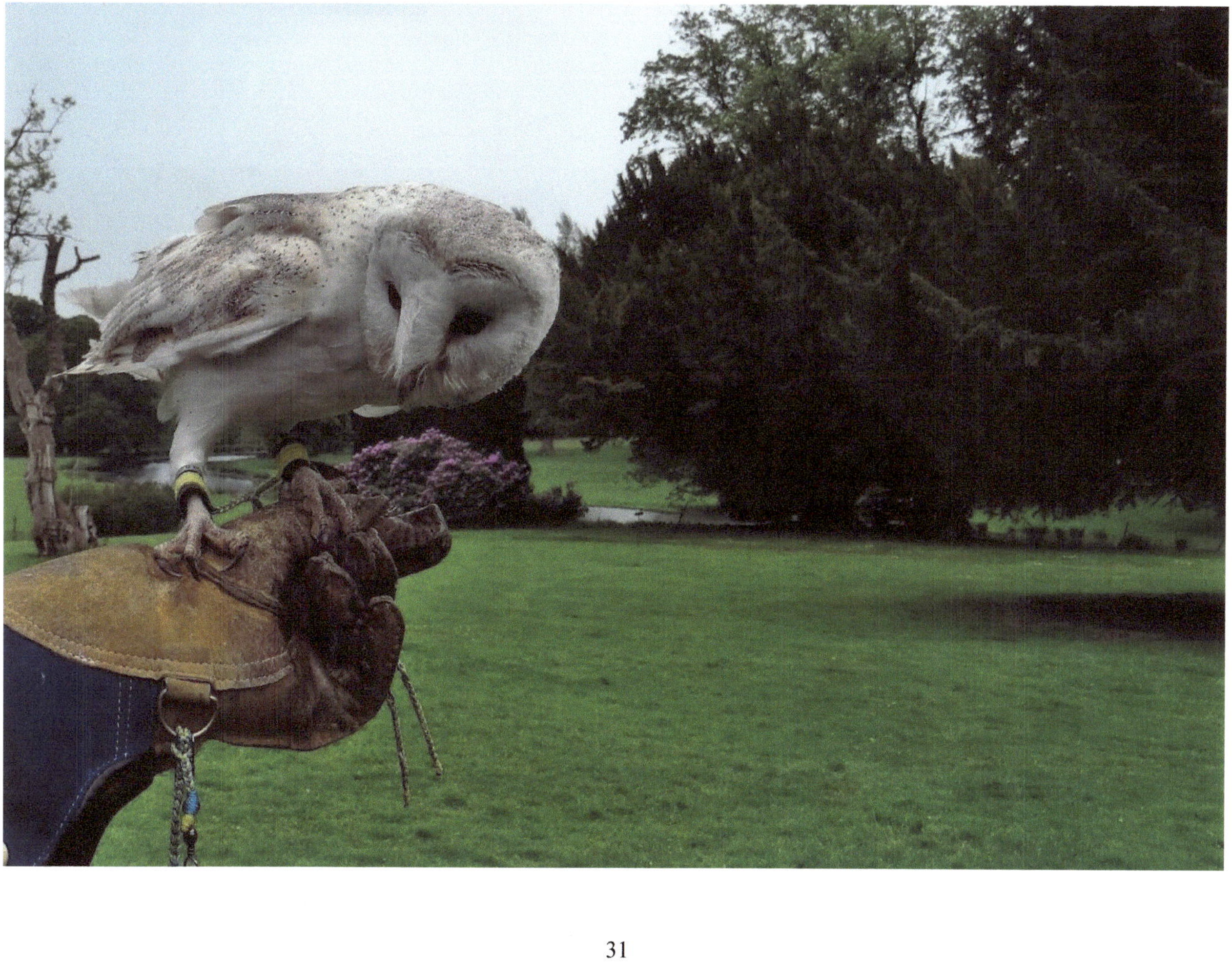

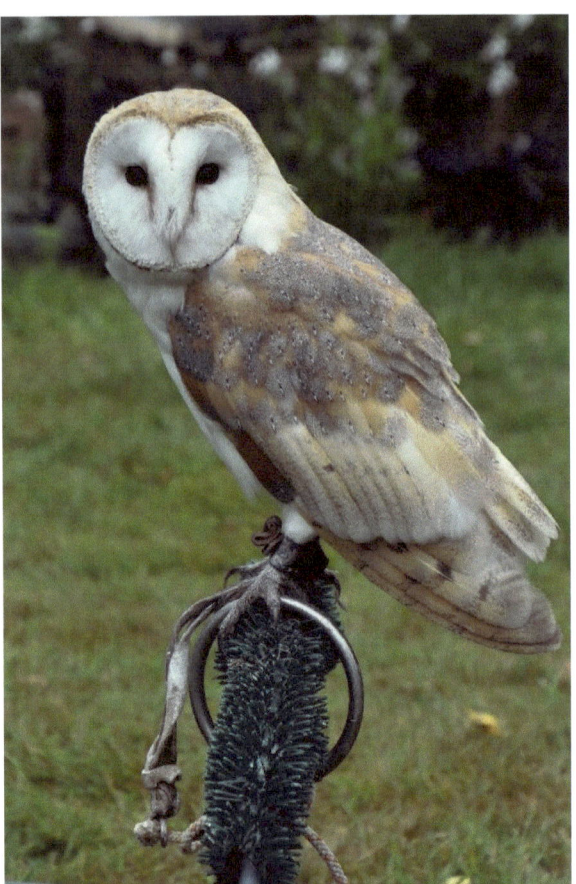
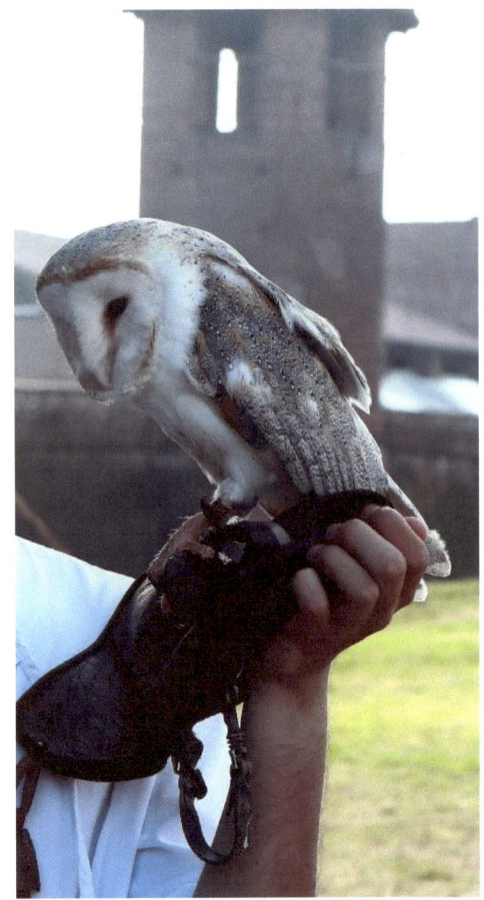
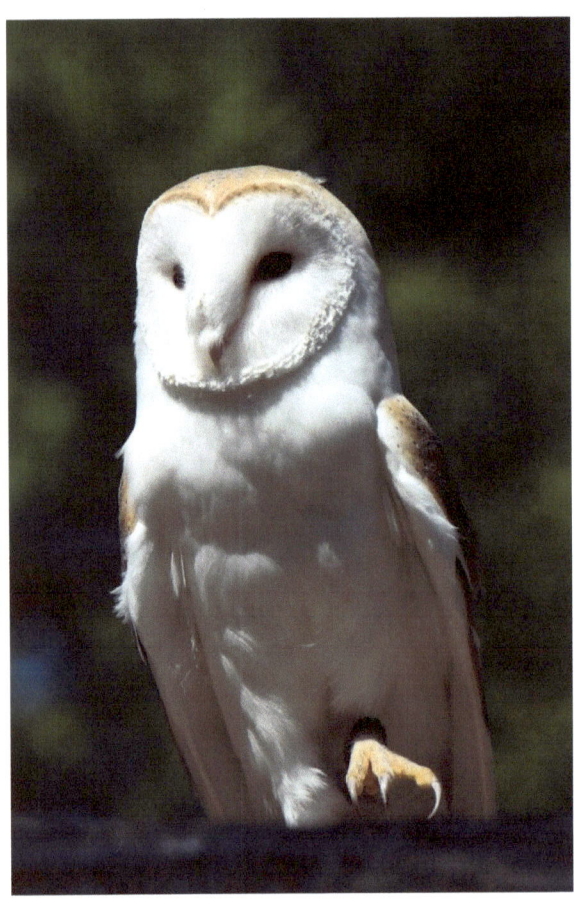
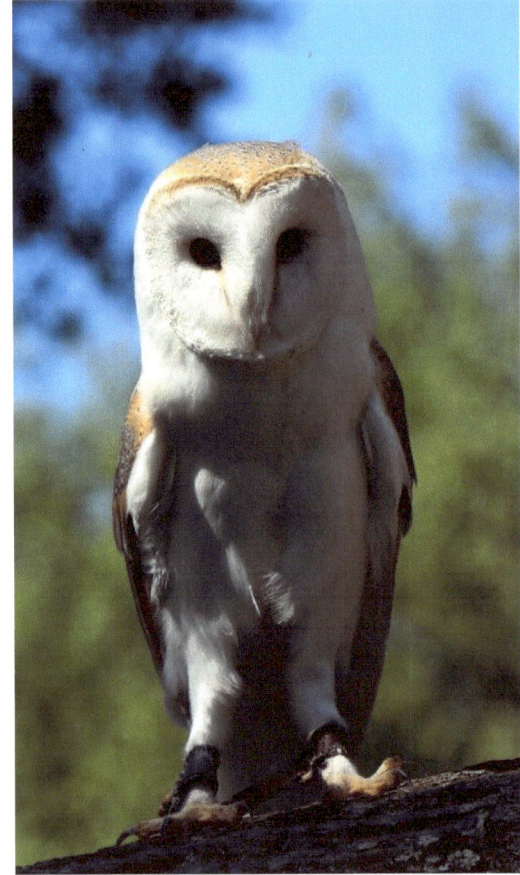

9 SLEEPY

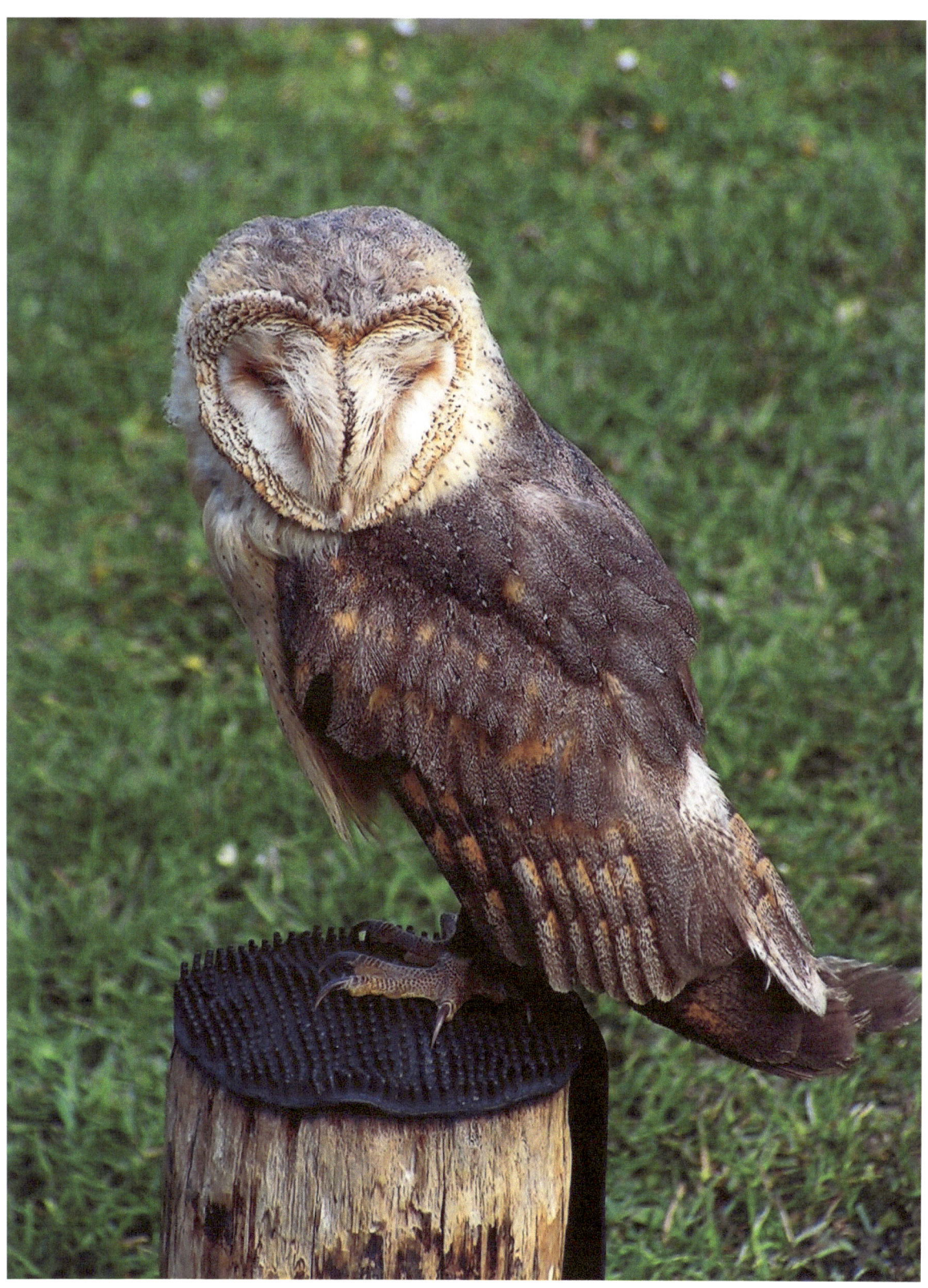

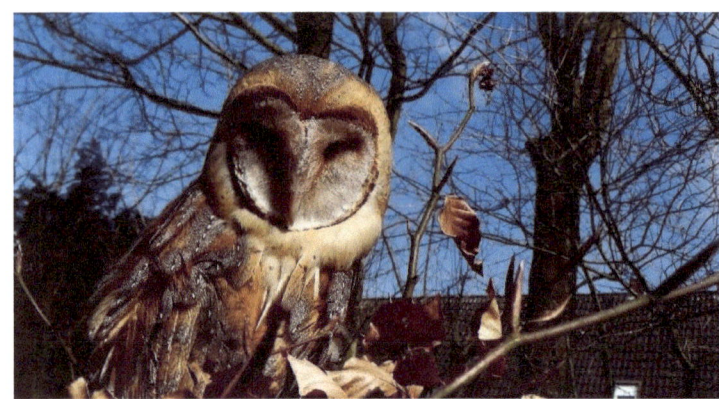
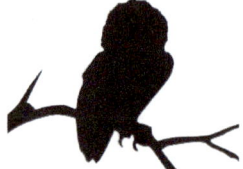
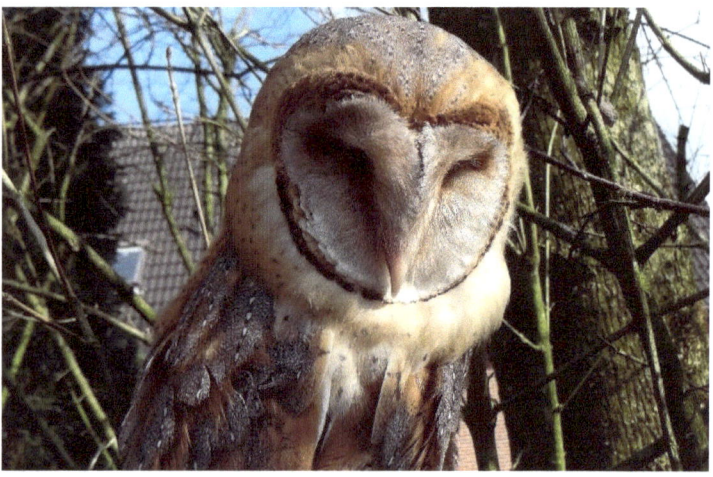
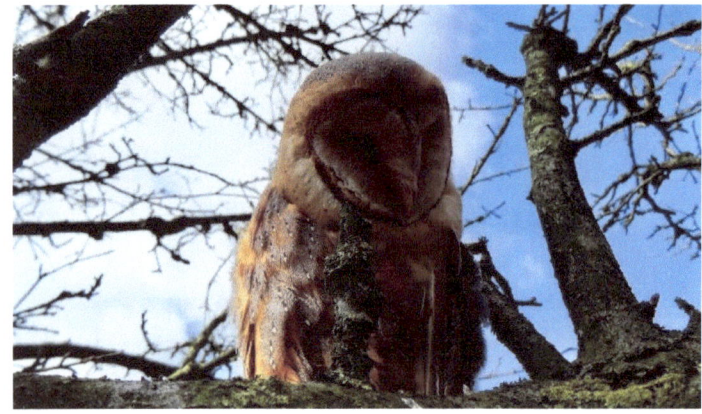
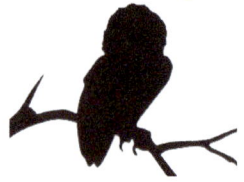
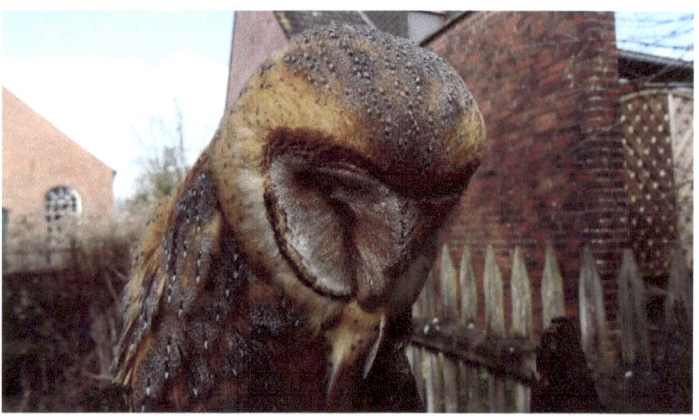

10 WINGS

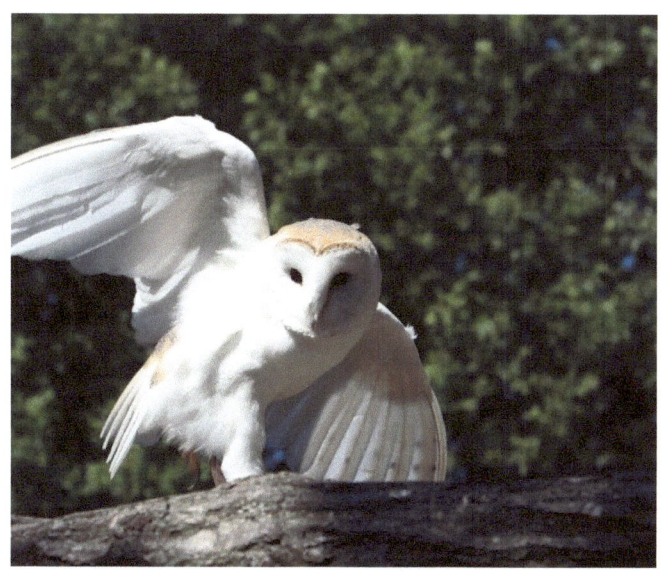

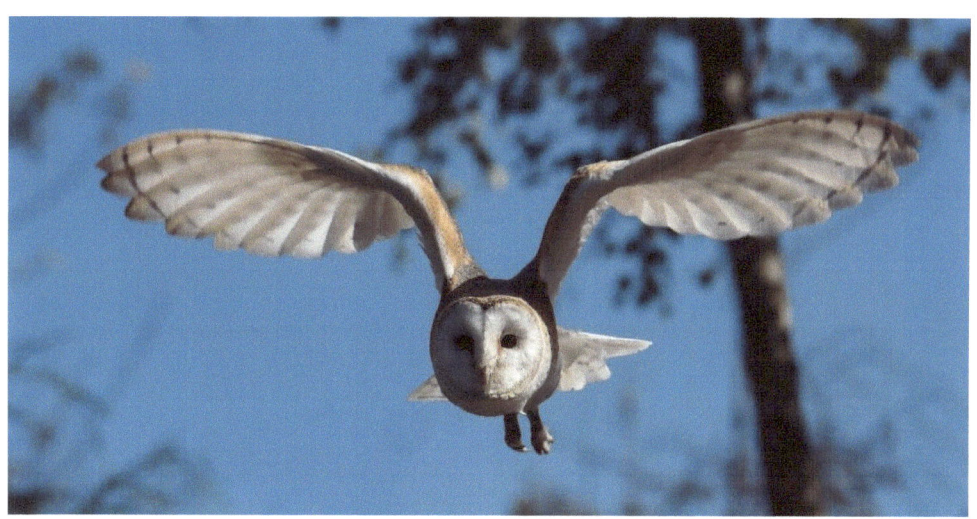

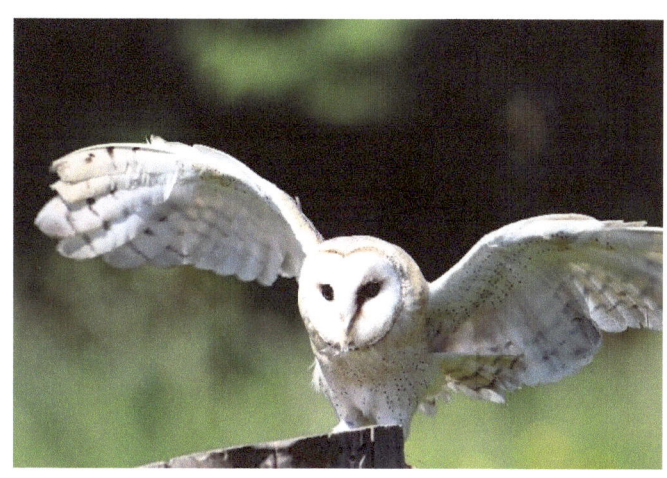

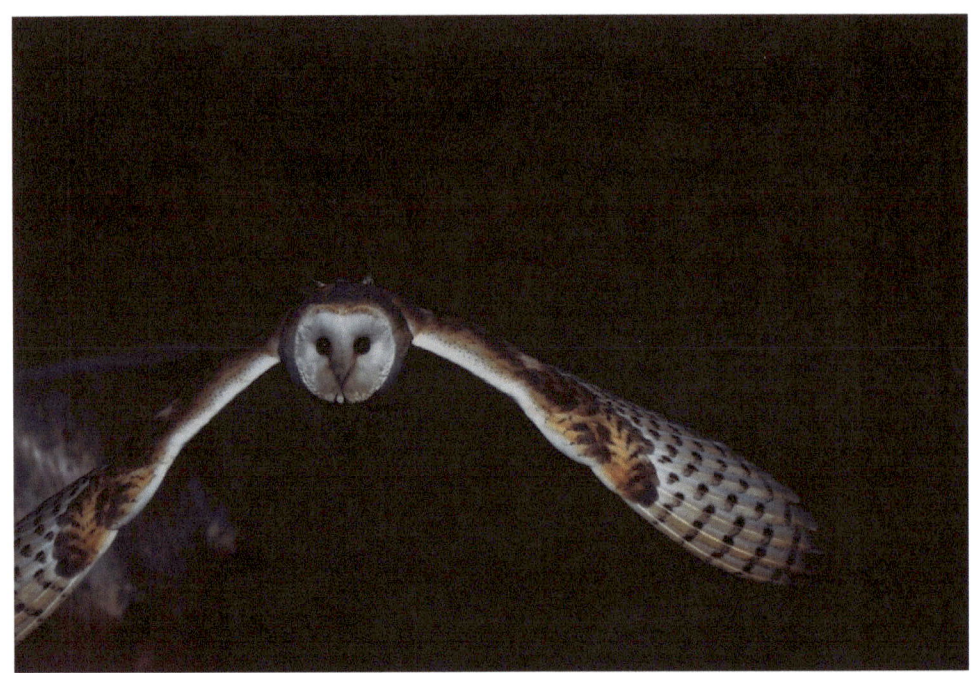
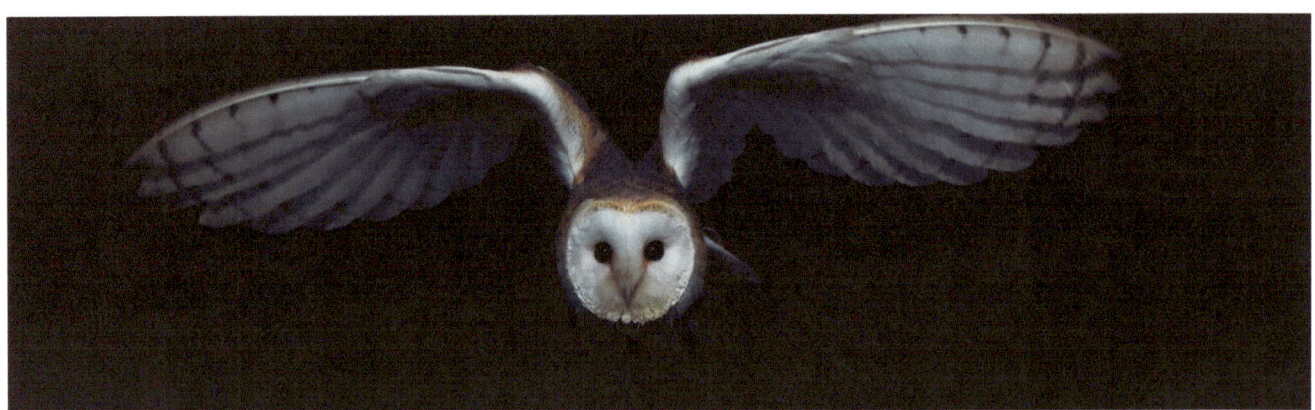
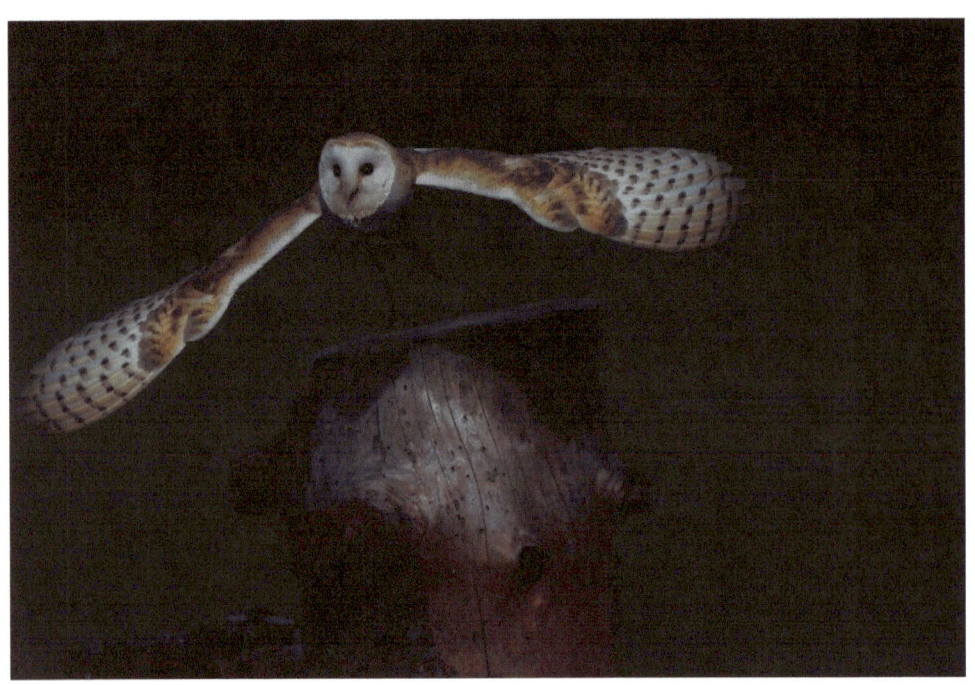

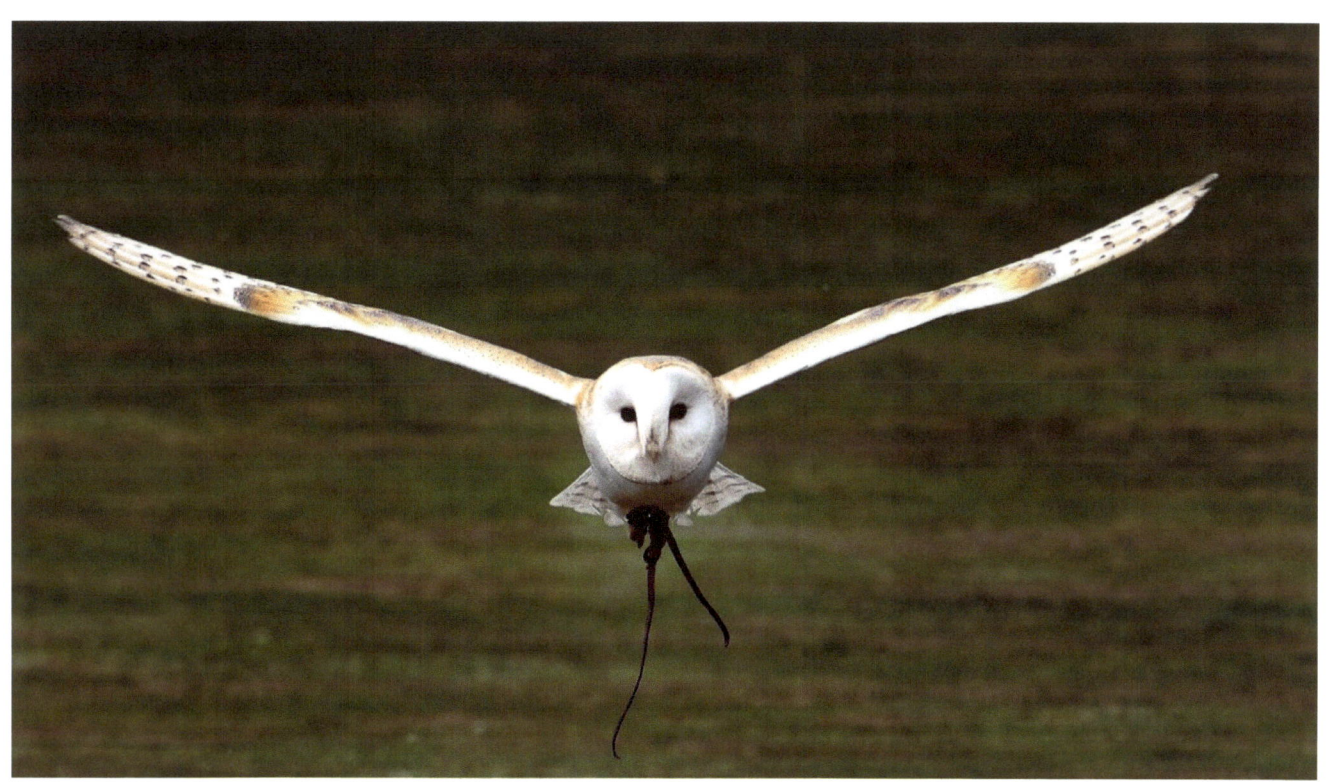

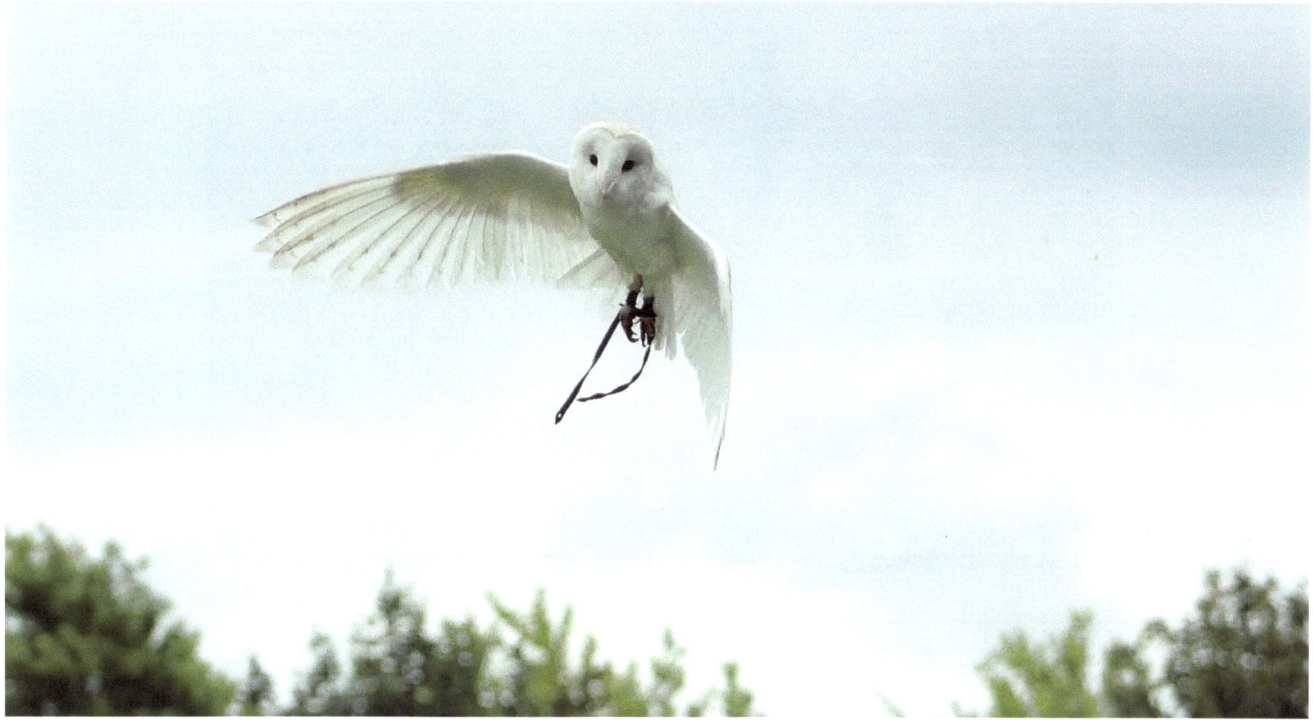

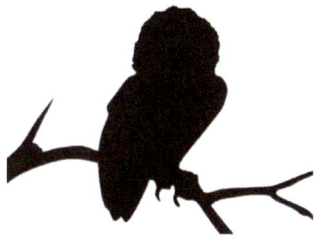

11 ARTWORK

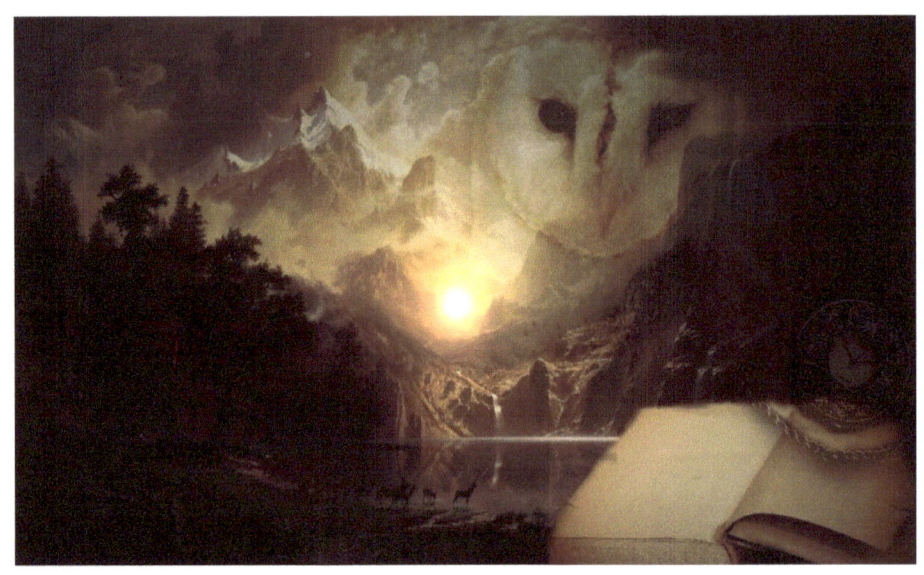

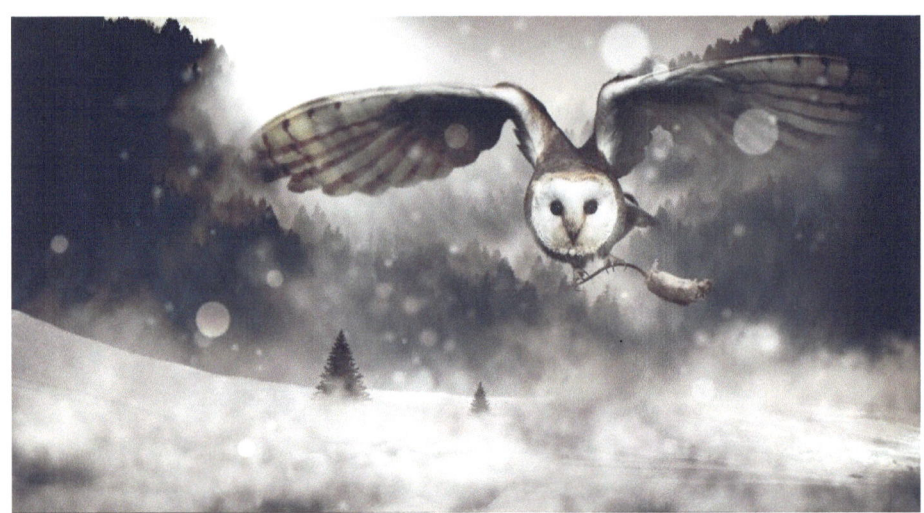

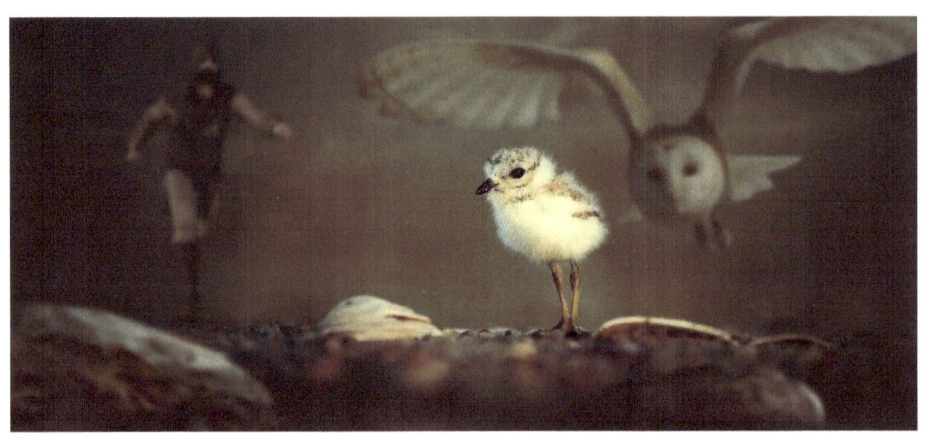

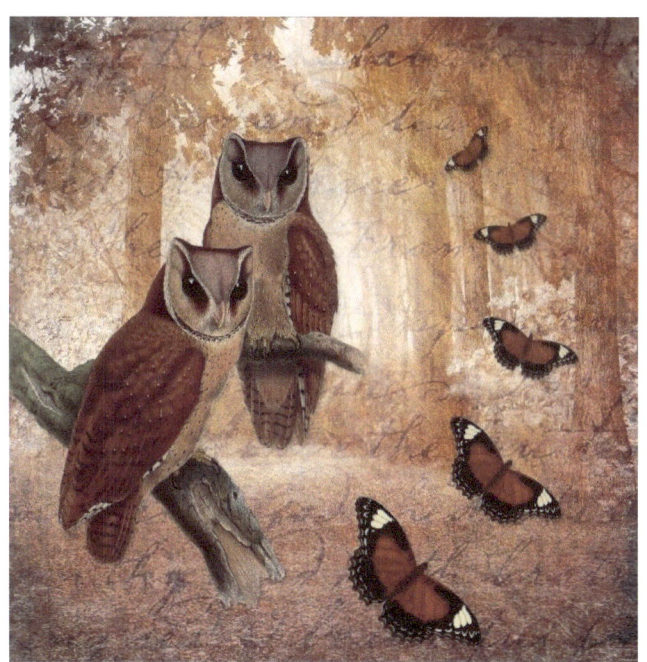
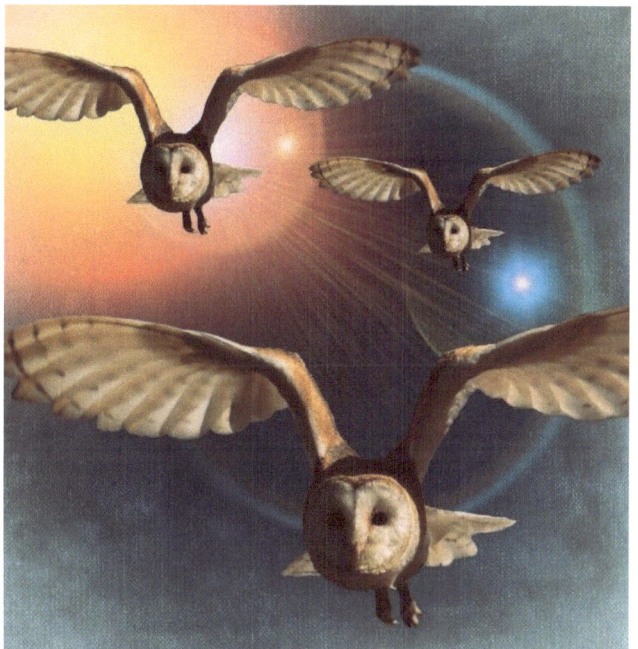
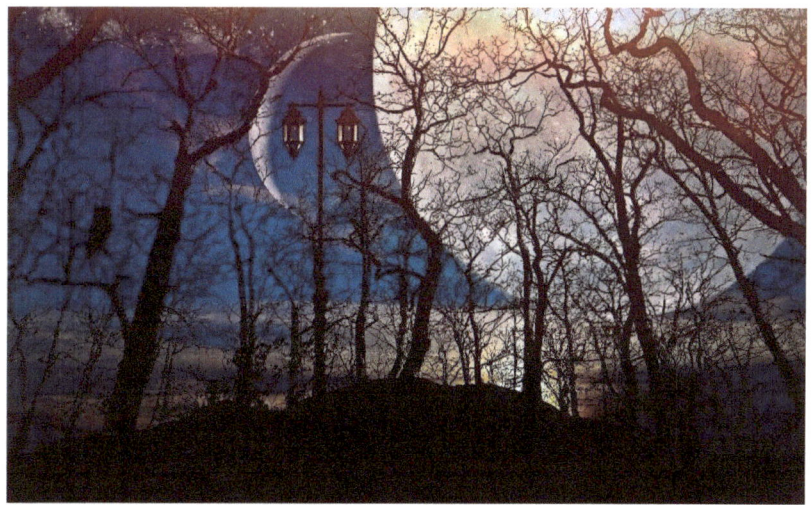
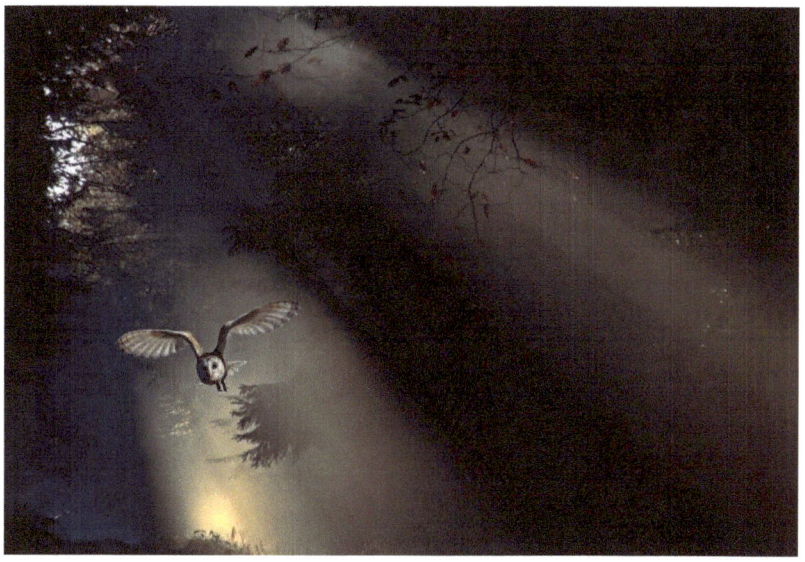

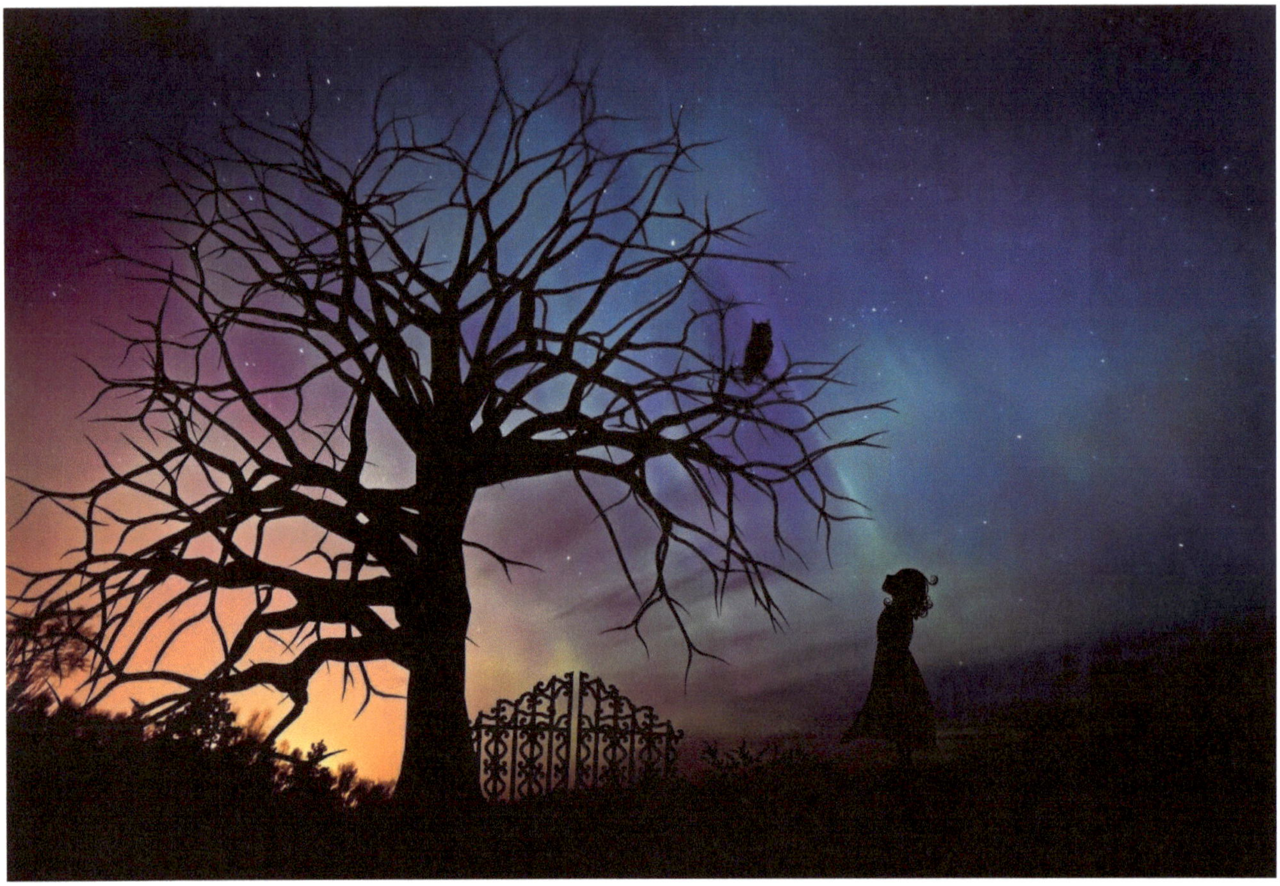

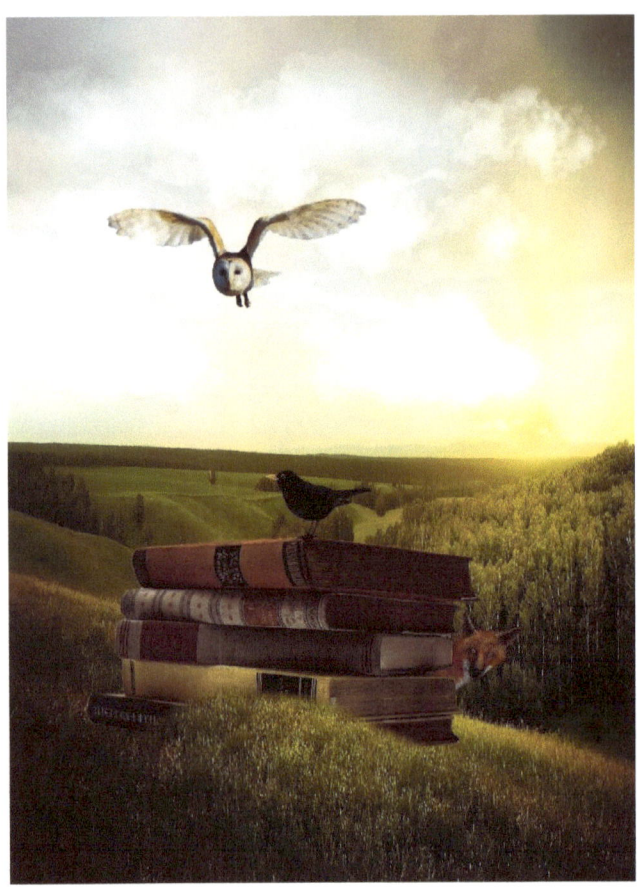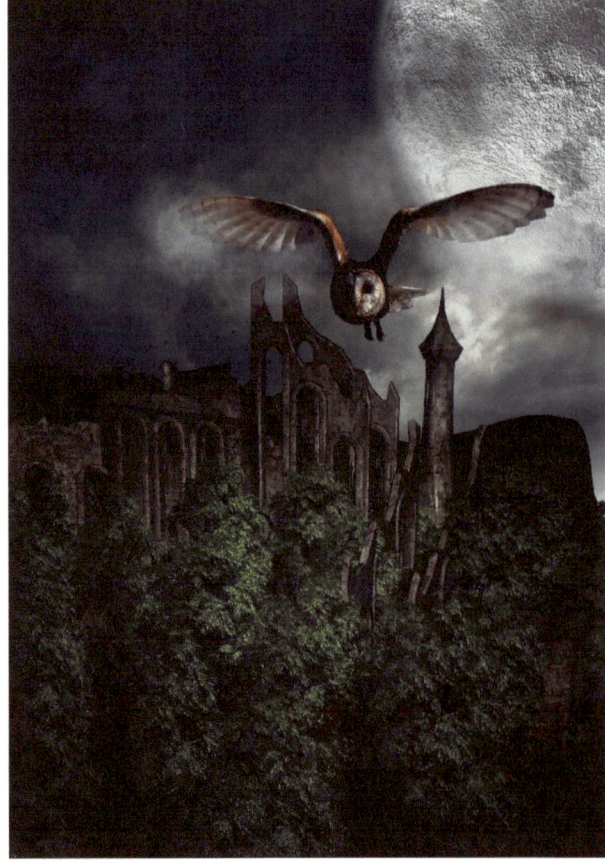

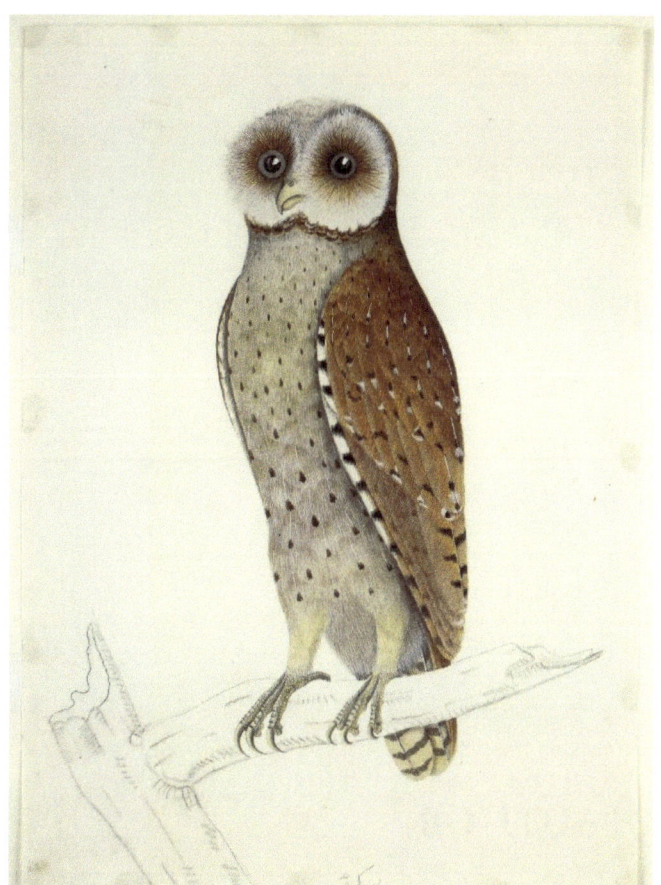
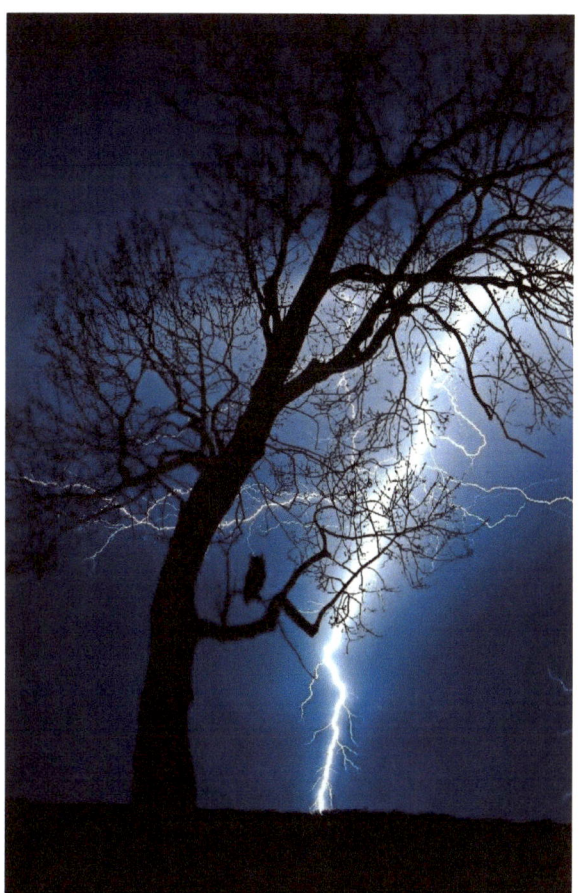
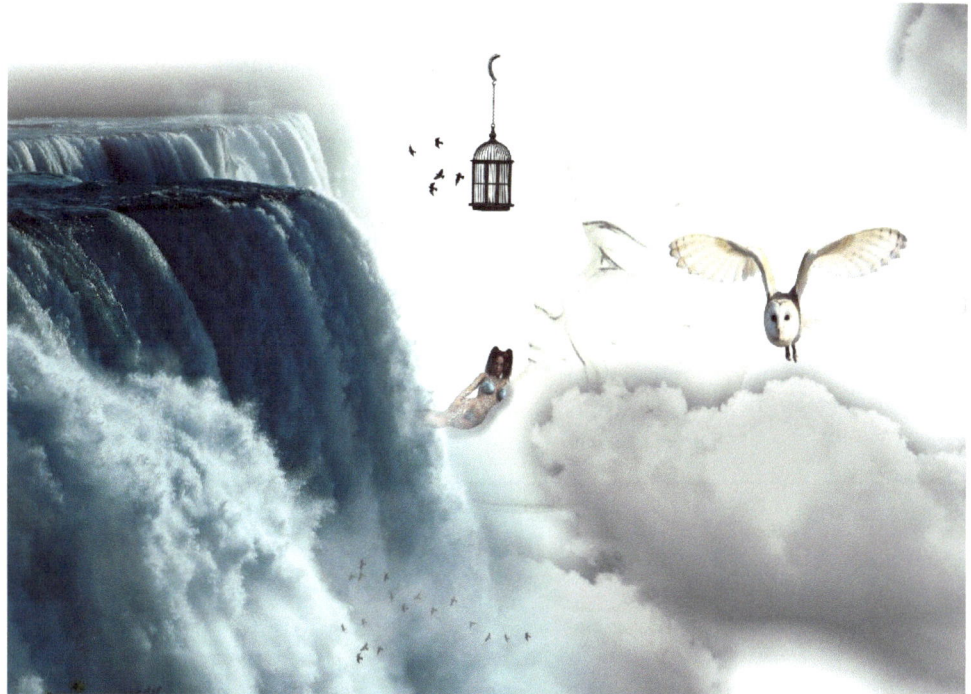

ABOUT THE AUTHOR

Sharon Buydens has written books on tiny houses, passive solar homes, green (eco-friendly) building and alternative construction, among other topics. This book is one in a series of picture books / photobooks that she has published. The author's website is www.sunstar-solutions.com

www.ingramcontent.com/pod-product-compliance
Lightning Source LLC
Chambersburg PA
CBHW042322250526
R18347200002B/R183472PG45473CBX00011B/13